Endorsements
The Secret

"Pastor and best-selling author .... the gospel material from a fresh—and at times radical—perspective. . . . He does an excellent job of capturing Jesus' quiet, revolutionary style."

—*Publishers Weekly* (starred review)

"In *The Secret Message of Jesus* Brian McLaren shares his own ferocious journey in pondering the teachings and actions of Jesus. As you read this terrific book, you may find yourself questioning Jesus, appreciating Jesus, admiring Jesus, and perhaps, in the end, feeling a sense of love and loyalty. What happens to you in the reading is not unlike what happened to the men and women who met Jesus thousands of years ago, and the millions who have claimed to have met him since. McLaren is surprisingly objective, and it is his lack of salesmanship or agenda that creates a refreshing picture of the man who claimed to be God."

— DONALD MILLER, Author of *Blue Like Jazz*

"In this critical book, Brian challenges us to ask what it would mean to truly live the message of Jesus today, and thus to risk turning everything upside down."

— JIM WALLIS, Author of *God's Politics* and editor of *Sojourners*

"Brian McLaren has given us an insightful, timely, and occasionally startling distillation of the message of Jesus. He is well aware of the many ways it has been distorted and debased by ourselves among others, but McLaren argues compellingly that it continues to be the best message we have—bringing clarity, guidance, and, above all, *hope* into our shadowed and floundering world."

— FREDERICK BUECHNER

"Here McLaren breaks new ground. *The Secret Message of Jesus* is his first decoding of the Gospel for those who are, or wish to be, 'a new kind of Christian.' More to the point, Christians of every kind, old or new, will receive energy and a renewal of their own commitment from reading these pages."

— PHYLLIS TICKLE, Religion editor (ret.) *Publishers Weekly* and compiler of *The Divine Hours*

"Brian McLaren insists gently that we recognize the message of Jesus as an ongoing revolution that may never come to an end in time. The Law of God doesn't change, no, but our perception of it is never static; it does and must change as the centuries pass. New study, new insights, new metaphors and new acknowledgements of past limitations can bring us closer and closer to the living, breathing, and dynamic nature of Scripture as we seek to meet its radical demands. McLaren reminds us that we have been invited to transform ourselves through Christ. Lucid, compelling, crucial and liberating: a book for those who seek to experience the blessed heat of Christianity at its source."

— ANNE RICE, Author of *Christ the Lord: Out of Egypt*

"In *The Secret Message of Jesus* the religious fog begins to lift and the revolutionary life that Jesus lived and calls us to begins to take shape. Take a chance on this wise and thought-provoking book."

— ZACH LIND, Drummer, Jimmy Eat World

"There is good reason that Brian McLaren is "emerging" as a prominent voice in the new shape of the church to come. His passion and gifts are fully articulated in this volume wherein he invites the reader back to the most urgent and elemental dimensions of Jesus. McLaren pushes beyond conventional church faith to the rawness of the text, there to be met by One who is revolutionary, subversive, and invitational in demanding and healing ways."

— WALTER BRUEGGEMANN, Professor, Columbia Theological Seminary, and author of *The Prophetic Imagination*

"This is the *real* "DaVinci Code"—the lost message to the contemporary church. A powerful, eye-opening book that has me rethinking my own position on everything."

— JACK HAFER, Film producer, *To End All Wars*

"Over the last few years Brian McLaren has helped so many of us navigate the changing landscape of our emerging post-modern culture. While bringing insight and hope to so many of the hard questions of belief our new world brings, his books have enabled us to reimagine the nature and purpose of our faith and the church. In *The Secret Message of Jesus*, Brian helps us further on our journey, with probably his most important work to date."

— JASON CLARK, Coordinator, Emergent-UK

"As I finished reading *The Secret Message of Jesus*, the thought came to mind that this is the last Christian book I need to read. It is time to set down the books and start *doing*."

— TIM BLAIR, Executive vice president, Parable Christian Stores

"It's amazing that the secret message of Jesus is also a secret to many Christians, but Brian McLaren courageously explains how and why this has happened. In this book, the "good news" sounds good again—to non-Christian and Christian alike."

— OTEIL BURBRIDGE, Bass player, The Allman Brothers Band

"Brian is thoughtful and probing and edgy and restless. Kind of like the guy he's writing about."

— JOHN ORTBERG, Best-selling author and teaching pastor,
Menlo Park Presbyterian Church

"Brian explores Jesus and his 'secret' message imaginatively, invitingly, and in ways certain to provoke controversy and conversation, just like Jesus did."

— DICK STAUB, President of The Center for Faith and Culture,
broadcaster, and author of *Christian Wisdom of the Jedi Masters*

"Brian McLaren has done it again! He has written a book that challenges traditional religiosity with a vital rediscovery of the central biblical truths."

— TONY CAMPOLO, Professor Emeritus, Eastern University, and author of *Speaking My Mind*

"This book will make you uncomfortable. It might make you mad. Jesus has that affect on people, Brian McLaren reminds us with understated wisdom. *The Secret Message of Jesus* challenges us to put aside our sterile certainties about Christ and reconsider the imaginative world of Jesus' stories, signs, and wonders."

— MARK MOSSA, S.J., Co-author of *Just War, Lasting Peace: What Christian Traditions Can Teach Us.*

"What Brian McLaren brings to the task of understanding and responding to the person, personality, and program of Jesus is an exceptional way of imagining. His gift is to bring together an intelligent reading of the gospels, an acute sensitivity to the beauty and brutality of humankind, and a compelling and far-reaching grasp of the possibilities inherent in Jesus' message. This book should renew our hope."

— ANDREW PERRIMAN, Author of *The Coming of the Son of Man*

THE
SECRET
MESSAGE OF
JESUS

Uncovering the Truth That Could
Change Everything

Brian D. McLaren

W Publishing Group
A Division of Thomas Nelson Publishers
Since 1798
www.wpublishinggroup.com

THE SECRET MESSAGE OF JESUS

Published by W Publishing Group, a Division of Thomas Nelson, Inc., P.O. Box 141000, Nashville, Tennessee 37214.

Names and details have been changed to respect the privacy of people whose personal stories are shared in this book.

Library of Congress Cataloging-in-Publication Data

McLaren, Brian D., 1956–
   The secret message of Jesus : uncovering the truth that could change everything / Brian McLaren.
     p.cm.
   ISBN 0-8499-0000-X (HC)
   ISBN 0-8499-9143-9 (IE)
   1. Jesus Christ—Person and offices. I. Title.
BT203.M37 2006
232.9'54—dc22   2005033686

Printed in the United States of America
06 07 08 09 10 RRD 9 8 7 6 5 4 3 2 1

CONTENTS

PART 3

IMAGINATION: EXPLORING HOW JESUS' SECRET MESSAGE COULD CHANGE EVERYTHING

INTRODUCTION

Seek first . . .
—MATTHEW 6:33

For many years, I have been seeking something. You might call it a spiritual quest or maybe a personal obsession. The goal of my exploration is to understand Jesus—and, in particular, his message. No, I don't think I can contain it in my little brain. It's not so much that I'm trying to get his great big message into my little head; it's more that I'm trying to get my little head fully into Jesus' message.

Some people think that a spiritual quest of any kind is a colossal waste of time. For them, the only things that are real are those that can be proven and measured. They might think, *Life boils down to earning and buying and selling . . . eating and drinking and having fun . . . respiration, digestion, elimination, ovulation, ejaculation, gestation, reproduction, antiquation, expiration. Why search for something that we can't prove? Why don't we just get real and get over it? Why waste energy on a spiritual quest? There's nothing more than psychology and biology, which is nothing more than chemistry and electricity, which is nothing but physics, which boils down to mathematics. That's all there is.*

Others think my search is a waste of time for a different reason. They think they've got Jesus and his message figured out, reduced to their own kind of mathematics. *It's these three concepts or those four steps or this simple little five-part formula—no more sophisticated than an elementary equation, really. It's 3 + 4 = 7. It's 16 − 9 = 7. It's −7 + 7 = 0. Why is Brian so misguided or difficult that he doesn't just repeat them and get with the program?*

But many people seem to share my hunch that neither a formulaic religious approach nor a materialistic secular approach has it all nailed down. Think of all the people who in recent years have read (or seen) *The Da Vinci Code*—not just as a popular page-turner but as an experience in shared frustration with the status-quo, male-dominated, power-oriented, cover-up-prone organized Christian religion. Why is the vision of Jesus hinted at in Dan Brown's book more interesting, more attractive, and more intriguing to these people than the standard version of Jesus they hear about from churches? Why would they be disappointed to find that Brown's version of Jesus has been largely discredited as fanciful and inaccurate, leaving only the church's conventional version? Is it possible that even though Brown's fictional version misleads in many ways, it at least serves to open up the possibility that the church's conventional versions of Jesus may not do him justice?

Think about all the people who have explored the Gnostic gospels in recent years, hoping to get a better, more radical vision of Jesus and his message. What if the problem isn't with our accepted stories of Jesus (the stories given us by Matthew, Mark, Luke, and John in contrast to these alternate accounts) but rather with our success at domesticating them and with our failure to see them in their native wildness and original vigor? What if, properly understood, the canonical (or accepted) Gospel of Matthew is far more radical and robust than the apocryphal Gospel of Thomas, or the canonical Gospel of John is far more visionary and transformative than the apocryphal Gospel of Peter—if only we "had ears to hear," as Jesus says?

Think about all the people who read articles or watch documentaries about Jesus on educational media every chance they get, hoping to get a deeper glimpse into this singularly fascinating personality. And think about the people who are repulsed by the usual cast of religious spokespeople on the nightly news or talk shows, not to mention paid religious broadcasting. To what degree are these communicators and communications media representing or misrepresenting Jesus and his message?

Think about the people who have profound spiritual experiences that tell them there's something more to life, something that can't be reduced to the formulas or mechanisms of organized religion or reductionist science. Think about the people who—even though they've given up on "organized religion" due to bad or boring experiences with it—still have a high opinion of Jesus. Or maybe "opinion" isn't the right word: what they have is a certain sense of *possibility* regarding Jesus, a sense that there might be more going on with him than most people realize, including perhaps many who call themselves Christians.

These unsatisfied people—and I'm one of them—have this unshakable intuition that both he and his message are better than anything they've heard or understood or figured out so far. They—I should say "we"—feel that there's a missing puzzle piece without which the big picture won't snap into place. There's a hidden door somewhere behind a curtain or bookcase, and through that door there are rooms we've never imagined.

They—we—have this hunch that there's a secret we don't yet get.

I'm not talking about something silly. I'm not talking about some kind of crazy conspiracy theory or wild speculation. I don't want to insult anybody, so I won't mention anything specific, but you know what I mean: I'm not talking about Jesus being in league with aliens from the planet Zorcon-3 or anything like that.

The secret I'm thinking of is more like the kind of rush of insight that comes to you near the end of a really good movie: you've been confused about something since the very first scene, but suddenly it all comes together. For many of us, we feel we've been watching the movie attentively, but we haven't gotten to that moment of clarity yet. We wish it would come.

I could tell you I've got it all figured out. But if I did, you probably wouldn't believe me anyway. After all, there's nothing more common than some religious kook claiming to have the final word!

No, I can't tell you that I have it all figured out, but I can tell you I am confident that I'm on to something. After many years of searching, struggling, questioning, doubting, wondering, walking away frustrated, returning, rereading, and starting all over again, I've seen a few things that are making the pieces come together for me and many others. If I'm not at that point in the movie where the rush of insight happens, I'm right on the verge of it. Maybe as I write the pages you're about to read, more will come clear and I'll cross the threshold to a new degree of understanding.

I hope so. That's why I'm writing. I assume that's why you're reading.

I'm envisioning three kinds of people as I write this book. First, you may never have heard of me or read any of my previous books. You're reading this sentence because of the title or the topic or the cover art or the recommendation of a friend, not because of the author. I'm glad we can in some way become acquainted through this book, and I hope you'll think some new thoughts and imagine new possibilities as you read. I hope the secret message of Jesus wins your heart as it has mine.

I'm especially hopeful that this book will be helpful to people who consider themselves spiritual but not religious, or interested in Jesus but not Christianity. Even though I've been a pastor for twenty-some years, I sympathize, as there is much in the religious establishment that repels me. That's one of the reasons I have looked forward so much to writing this book: I believe the secret message of Jesus provides a clear alternative and a different direction than our religious establishments frequently take.

Second, you may have read one or more of my previous books and decided to take a risk on another. You may feel, as I do, that my previous books have been clearing the ground for something new—and you have a hunch this book might contain the seed of that "something new."

Third, some people have considered my previous writings controversial (or worse), and some readers may come from their number. If this describes you, I hope you will find something of value here; I know you will find weaknesses to point out. For example, you may wish I had said more on particular dimensions of Jesus' message or life that are of special importance to you.[1] I trust you will keep three things in mind. First, I didn't feel a need to cover ground here that many other authors have already covered quite well. Second, I decided it would be better to write a shorter book that people might finish than a longer book that would scare them away. Third, my focus here is Jesus' message—not how Jesus fits into this or that systematic theology, as important as that subject might be to some folk. Thoughtful critics will realize I'm aiming for a broad, nonscholarly, and in many cases nonreligious audience and sometimes have to take a path that's not ideal for either the highly knowledgeable or the newly curious.[2]

Here's what to expect in this book. In part 1, we'll look at Jesus and his times. We'll try to understand him against the backdrop of politics, religion, and the social dreams and pain of his day. In part 2, we'll look more closely at Jesus' message itself—first by taking seriously the various media that carried his message and then by immersing ourselves in his message. Finally, having gone back and saturated ourselves in Jesus' message, in part 3, we'll return to our own time, our own world with all its problems and challenges and opportunities, and we'll try to see our world in a fresh light.

If we succeed in grasping even some fragment of Jesus' secret message, if we take it in and manage not only to look *at* it but also to learn to look *through* it, our world and our lives will look different to us at the end of our exploration. And if that happens deeply enough for enough of us, everything could change.

PART I

EXCAVATION:

DIGGING BENEATH THE SURFACE TO UNCOVER JESUS' MESSAGE

CHAPTER I

TROUBLING QUESTIONS ABOUT JESUS

Are you still so dull?

—MATTHEW 15:16

What if Jesus of Nazareth was right—more right, and right in different ways, than we have ever realized? What if Jesus had a message that truly could change the world, but we're prone to miss the point of it?

What if we have developed a religion that makes reverent and honoring statements about Jesus but doesn't teach what Jesus taught in the manner he taught it? What if the religion generally associated with Jesus neither expects nor trains its adherents to actually live in the way of Jesus?

What if the core message of Jesus has been unintentionally misunderstood or intentionally distorted? What if many have sincerely valued some aspects of Jesus' message while missing or even suppressing other, more important dimensions? What if many have carried on a religion that faithfully celebrates Jesus in ritual and art, teaches about Jesus in sermons and books, sings about Jesus in songs and hymns, and theorizes about Jesus in seminaries and classrooms . . . but somewhere along the way missed rich and radical treasures hidden in the essential message of Jesus?

What if too many of today's religious leaders—among whom I must be counted—are among the last to get the message of Jesus and the first to reduce, oppose, distort, or suppress it, just as they did in Jesus' day?

What if Jesus had actually concealed his deepest message, not trying to make it overt and obvious but intentionally hiding it as a treasure one must seek in order to find? If that's the case, why would Jesus ever do such a thing? How would we find his message if he had indeed hidden it?

What if Jesus' secret message reveals a secret plan? What if he didn't come to start a new religion—but rather came to start a political, social, religious, artistic, economic, intellectual, and spiritual revolution that would give birth to a new world?[1]

What if his secret message had practical implications for such issues as how you live your daily life, how you earn and spend money, how you treat people of other races and religions, and how the nations of the world conduct their foreign policy? What if his message directly or indirectly addressed issues like advertising, environmentalism, terrorism, economics, sexuality, marriage, parenting, the quest for happiness and peace, and racial reconciliation?

Would we want to know what that message is? How much? Would we be willing to look hard, think deeply, and search long in order to find it? Would we be willing to rethink our assumptions?

What if the message of Jesus was good news—not just for Christians but also for Jews, Buddhists, Muslims, Hindus, New Agers, agnostics, and atheists? And what if the message of Jesus also contained warnings—for Jews, Buddhists, Muslims, Hindus, New Agers, agnostics, atheists—and for Christians too? What difference could it make in the lives of individuals, in their families and neighborhoods and circles of friends, and in the world at large? Those are the questions we're going to explore in these pages.

For me, these aren't just theoretical questions. I grew up in the church and heard wonderful stories about Jesus that captured my imagination throughout my childhood. Then in my teenage years, after a brief but intense period of doubt, I became intrigued by Jesus in a more mature way, and I began wondering what it means to be an authentic follower of Jesus in my daily life. In college and graduate school, although I went through times of questioning, skepticism, and disillusionment, I retained confidence that Jesus himself was somehow right and real and from God—even if the religions bearing his name seemed to be a very mixed bag and adherents like me often set a disappointing example.

After graduate school, I worked as an English instructor at a large secular university, and I tried to relate what I knew of Jesus to the world of higher education. In the mid-1980s, I left higher education and entered pastoral ministry, where I have spent the last twenty years of my life, serving in a church just outside Washington, D.C. As a pastor and as a human being, I have had one lasting obsession: the fascinating, mysterious, uncontainable, uncontrollable, enigmatic, vigorous, surprising, stunning, dazzling, subtle, honest, genuine, and explosive personality of Jesus.

But through these years, an uncomfortable feeling has showed me that the portrait of Jesus I found in the New Testament didn't fit with the image of Christianity projected by religious institutions, charismatic televangelists, religious spokespeople in the media—and sometimes, my own preaching. Sometimes the discomfort has come when I realize that Jesus' teachings and example don't fit neatly in the categories of my theology. Sometimes the discomfort has risen from the simple, sad fact that even though I identify myself as a Christian, I'm too often a shabby jerk; and as much as I want to change, I stubbornly stay stuck in old patterns, wishing for more transformation than I've experienced so far.

So I've been on a journey, a search. You might call it a journey of doubt, because I've doubted some conventional understandings of Jesus and his message. You might also call it a journey of faith, because my quest emerges from deep conviction that whatever the essential meaning of Jesus' message is, it's true and worth knowing—that even if it overturns some of our conventional assumptions, priorities, values, and practices, a better understanding will be worth the temporary discomfort.

A lot of people say, "It doesn't matter what you believe, as long as you're sincere." They're partly right: sincerity is a precious thing, and arguments about who has the correct beliefs have too often led to arrogance, ugly arguments, and even violence. But believing untrue things, however sincerely, can have its own unintended consequences.

For example, try believing that God will be pleased if you fly an airplane into a tall building, that you can get away with embezzling funds, that you have a personal exemption from sexual propriety, or that your race or religion makes you superior to members of other races or religions. You will become someone nobody respects, including (eventually) you.

But seeking to believe what is true—seeking to see things as closely as possible to the way they really are, seeking to be faithful to what is and was and will be—puts you increasingly in touch with reality and helps you become a wise and good person. It can also make life a lot more meaningful, and enjoyable. For example, if you have a huge inheritance in the bank and don't believe it, or if somebody really loves you and you don't believe it, you're missing out on a lot, right? Having truer beliefs—beliefs more aligned with reality—makes all the difference.

In one of my previous books, I said that clarity is sometimes overrated and that intrigue is correspondingly undervalued. But here I want to say—clearly—that it is tragic for anyone, especially anyone affiliated with the religion named after Jesus, not to be clear about what Jesus' message actually was.

Many people don't realize that the Christian religion—in its Catholic, Protestant, Orthodox, and Pentecostal forms—is the largest, richest, and most powerful religion in the world. If the Christian religion "misunderestimates" the message of Jesus—if it doesn't know or believe the truth about Jesus and his message—the whole world will suffer from Christian ignorance, confusion, or delusion. But if it discovers, understands, believes, and lives Jesus' message—if it becomes increasingly faithful to the reality of what Jesus taught in word and example—then everyone could benefit: Christians, Jews, Muslims, Hindus, Buddhists, agnostics, atheists, everyone.

In an age of global terrorism and rising religious conflict, it's significant to note that all Muslims regard Jesus as a great prophet, that many Hindus are willing to consider Jesus as a legitimate manifestation of the divine, that many Buddhists see Jesus as one of humanity's most enlightened people, and that Jesus himself was a Jew, and (this book asserts) without understanding his Jewishness, one doesn't understand Jesus. A shared reappraisal of Jesus' message could provide a unique space or common ground for urgently needed religious dialogue—and it doesn't seem an exaggeration to say that the future of our planet may depend on such dialogue.[2] This reappraisal of Jesus' message may be the only project capable of saving a number of religions, including Christianity, from a number of threats, from being co-opted by consumerism or nationalism to the rise of potentially violent fundamentalism in their own ranks.

Wouldn't it be interesting if the people who started discovering and believing the hidden message of Jesus were people who aren't even identified as Christians, and wouldn't it be tragic if people like myself, identified as Christians, were unwilling to consider the possibility that they have more to learn (and unlearn) about the message of Jesus?

It might sound audacious of me even to suggest such a thing. But I speak from personal experience: I grew up in the church and spent many years in devout Christian contexts before I ever got more than a tiny glimpse of the secret message of Jesus. Even now, I feel I only see part of it; I feel like a child standing on the North Rim of the Grand Canyon—impressed, breathless, and maybe a little dizzy, but not able to take in the full dimensions of what expands before me. That is why I'm writing this book: not just for your benefit, but for mine as well.

So for all these reasons, I'd like to share my search with you and invite you to be part of it. I don't want to spoil the ending, but I'll let you in on this: the further I go on this search, the more inspired, moved, challenged, shocked, and motivated I become about the secret message of Jesus.

CHAPTER 2

THE POLITICAL
MESSAGE OF JESUS

The time is fulfilled, and the kingdom of God is at hand.
—MARK 1:15 ESV

I live near Washington, D.C. I've lived here nearly all my life,
so I guess it's not surprising that my investigation would
begin with the political dimension of Jesus' message. But I didn't
always see Jesus' message as political, and I never would have
considered the political dimension the best place to begin an
exploration like this. For most of my life, I was like an American
pastor I heard about when I was visiting London in 2004.

This American-born pastor was being interviewed on British
television. The interviewer asked him why so many Christians in
America unquestioningly supported the U.S. war in Iraq, when
that foreign policy (the interviewer felt) was so clearly against
the teachings of Jesus. The American pastor seemed surprised
and a little offended, so the interviewer explained, "Jesus talked
about peace and reconciliation, turning the other cheek, walking
the second mile, that sort of thing. How do you reconcile that

with your war?" The pastor hesitated a moment and then replied, "Well, the teachings of Jesus are personal. They have nothing to do with politics and foreign policy." When I heard this story, a chill crept up my neck as I remembered saying similar things myself many years ago. Whatever you think about war in general and the Iraq war in particular, questions about the public dimensions of Jesus' teachings are worth asking.

I've become convinced that although Jesus' message *was* personal, it *was not* private.[1] I've been convinced that it has everything to do with public matters in general and politics in particular—including economics and aid, personal empowerment and choice, foreign policy and war. The fact is, Jesus called his message *good news*, itself a public term that evoked the political announcements of the Roman emperors. When they would win an important military victory, they would send out messengers to announce *good news*.[2] Caesar Augustus, for example, who ruled the empire from 27 BC to AD 14, articulated his good news in this inscription found in Myra, Lycia: "Divine Augustus Caesar, son of god, imperator of land and sea, the benefactor and savior of the whole world, has brought you peace."

I've become convinced that if the *good news* of Jesus were carried in a newspaper today, it wouldn't be hidden in the religion section (although it would no doubt cause a ruckus there). It would be a major story in every section, from world news (What is the path to peace, and how are we responding to our neighbors in need?) to national and local news (How are we treating children, poor people, minorities, the last, the lost, the least? How are we treating our enemies?), in the lifestyle section (Are we loving our neighbors and throwing good parties to bring people together?), the food section (Do our diets reflect concern for God's planet and our poor neighbors, and have we invited any of them over for dinner lately?), the entertainment and sports sections (What is the point of our entertainment, and what values are we strengthening in sports?), and even the business section (Are we serving the wrong master: money rather than God?).

In my religious upbringing, I was not taught the public and political dimensions of Jesus' message—only the personal, private dimensions. Yes, Jesus loved me and wanted me to be good to my little brother and obedient to my parents. But Jesus' idea that God loves my nation's enemies, and so our foreign policies should reflect that love—that idea never crossed my mind. At some point, though, I began to get a hint that I was missing something. At that same moment, I think I began to catch a faint scent of the secret message of Jesus.

How did my thinking change to see the public and political dimensions of Jesus' message? My first answer would be that it came through reading the Bible. But that answer doesn't suffice, because for years I had read the Bible as millions of people do, oblivious to the message's public and political dimensions. Why for so long didn't I see what I eventually began to see? (More on this in appendix 1.)

Looking back, I'd say that my approach to reading the Bible—my assumptions and focus, what we could call my "interpretive grid"—helped me see some things and blinded me to or diverted me from others. What then changed my interpretive grid? That change came largely through two sources. First, I have had the pleasure of talking about the Bible to many people who had never read it before; their honest questions forced me to question some of my unexamined assumptions. Second, I have had the pleasure of reading and meeting theologians and historians who pointed out the historical and political context of the Bible that I'd been missing. When I learned some basic information about Jesus' historical and political context, from that new vantage point, a dynamic new picture began to take shape.[3]

That's why I'd like to launch our journey into Jesus' message by situating us in the political and social landscape into which Jesus was born and in which he lived, spoke, and launched a global spiritual revolution.

For starters, Jesus was Jewish. (No, he wasn't a Christian. Christianity as a separate religion didn't exist until well after Jesus died.) The Jewish people had been under foreign occupation and oppression for centuries. Since 586 BC, a succession of empires—the Assyrians, the Babylonians, the Medo-Persians, the Greeks, and the Romans—had ruled over them.

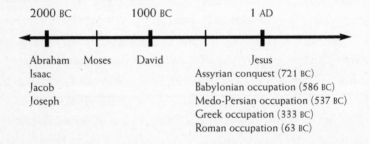

The Jewish people probably felt about their occupiers the way Palestinians generally feel today about the Israelis. They wanted to be free, to live in their own land without outside interference, occupation, and domination. In particular, it seemed wrong to the Jews, deeply wrong, that pagan nations would rule over a people who believed in the one true and living God. Why would the people with wrong, false religions rule over those with the right, true religion? The question intensified all the more when the Roman emperors like "the Divine Augustus Caesar" proclaimed themselves as gods, fusing what we would call church and state in a strong and frightening alloy. "How can we remain quiet and compliant citizens when our government is divinizing itself?" they would ask.

These questions elicited various answers. One group, known

as the Zealots, said, "The reason we're oppressed is that we're passive and cowardly. If we would have courage, if we would rise up
and rebel, God would give us victory. If we would take action and
slit a few Roman throats, if we had the faith and nerve to launch
a violent revolution, God would give us the power, like little
David, to defeat the Goliath that is Rome so we would be free."

Another group, the Herodians (named for supporters of the
puppet ruler, Herod, and joined by a party called the Sadducees),
thought the Zealots' approach was stupid and wrong. "You have
no idea how powerful Rome is. To rebel is suicide. Resistance is
futile; you will be crushed. No, we should make the best of our
situation, cooperate, and play the game. That's the only safe and
sensible way."

Another group, the Essenes, thought both Zealots and Herodians were unenlightened. They said, "The only way to please
God is to leave the corrupt religious and political systems and
create an alternative society out in the desert." They established
various wilderness communes where they sought to be faithful
by isolating themselves from the culture at large, which they felt
was sick beyond remedy.

A fourth group, the Pharisees, had a different diagnosis and
prescription: "The Lord would send Messiah to deliver us if we
would just become purer. If we would obey the Bible's teachings
more rigorously, God would liberate us. There's too much sin
and not enough piety among us. If there were more righteous
people like us and fewer sinners among us—fewer prostitutes,
drunks, and Roman collaborators—then Roman domination
would be brought to an end by God. It's the fault of those notorious sinners that we remain under the heel of the Roman boot!
Religious purity and rigor—that's the answer!"

Much as political parties today vie for power, these groups
argued, acted, and counteracted. Alliances and hostilities would

form and dissolve, re-form, and dissolve again. The Zealots would engage in some form of terrorism; the Herodians would decry their actions and swear greater allegiance to Rome. The Pharisees would scold the Zealots and Herodians alike and then launch into an attack on drunks and prostitutes with vigorous hellfire rhetoric. The Essenes, withdrawn from the fray out in the desert, would write strange literature expressing their disdain, perhaps secretly wishing that God would destroy the whole lot of them.

The question on everyone's minds, then, was something like this: "What should we do about the political and social mess we're in? Which path is the right path to take? How can we be liberated from the empire of Caesar, the empire of Rome?" I think you'll agree: those are public and political questions.

It's against this political backdrop that a carpenter's son named Jesus begins preaching.

Imagine a busy street crowded with people. A young man has gathered a crowd in a corner of the local market. Someone shouts out, "What's your plan? What's your message?"

He responds, "Change your way of thinking. The kingdom of God is available to all. Believe this good news! The empire of God is now available to all!"

The kingdom of God, the empire of God? What could Jesus mean by this? One thing is sure: he did not mean what many—perhaps most—people today think he meant. He did not mean "heaven after you die." Maybe the meaning would be clearer if we paraphrased it like this: "You're all preoccupied with the oppressive empire of Caesar and the oppressed kingdom of Israel. You're missing the point: the kingdom of God is here now, available to all! This is the reality that matters most. Believe this good news and follow me!"

If you're a first-century Jew, it's obvious to you that Jesus hasn't appeared in a vacuum. He isn't delivering lectures or debating with scholars at a theological seminary (although at the age of twelve he did spend a few days doing something like that in the temple in Jerusalem). He's preaching on the streets, in fields, out in public—because his message is a timely, public message. So you're standing there in the crowd, thinking, *Well, maybe he's a Zealot. It takes a lot of courage to stand up in public and speak out.*

Imagine that a Roman soldier comes along just then and disperses the crowd with an angry shout and a wave of his spear. Jesus doesn't call on the crowds to kill the infidel occupier; he, with the rest of the crowd, quietly complies. You feel disappointed. You were hoping to hear more of what this Galilean carpenter had to say. A few days later, you hear that he's speaking to a large crowd outside of town on a hillside. You rush out to hear him.

"Do you want to know who will be blessed? Not the powerful ones with lots of money and weapons. No, the poor will be blessed. Not the ones who can shout the loudest and get their way. No, the meek will be blessed. Not the ones who kill their enemies. No, the ones who are persecuted for doing what's right. Not those who play it safe, but those who stand up for the sake of justice. Not the clever and the sly, but the pure in heart. Not those who make war. No, those who make peace."

You say to yourself, "Well, he sounds like a Zealot in some ways, but he can't be a Zealot; they're all about power and violence, not peacemaking and meekness. And it's clear he's not an Essene, because they wouldn't even bother preaching to the rest of us. We're all lost causes in their minds, so they've retreated into their elite religious communes in the countryside. And he can't be a Herodian. They would never use inflammatory language like 'the kingdom of God,' and they wouldn't talk about standing up against injustice. They would say that God wants us to honor the emperor and sit down and be quiet. So I'm not sure just where he fits in. Maybe he's a Pharisee."

But a few minutes later, Jesus says, "You must be more just and good than the Pharisees are. They just wash the outside of the cup; they don't deal with the inside. The Pharisees won't enter the kingdom of God. If you want to enter it, you must surpass the Pharisees in your pursuit of goodness. Even the prostitutes will enter the kingdom of God before the Pharisees will!"

That shocks you. How could anyone be more just and better than a Pharisee? They follow the rules scrupulously. And how could anyone dare to antagonize the Pharisees? After all, they have a reputation for responding severely to those who disagree with them. Maybe Jesus represents some sort of new super-Pharisee movement—maybe he's trying to out-Pharisee the Pharisees. But then you see Jesus at a party a few nights later. Attending this party are prostitutes, drunks, Roman collaborators (tax collectors), and other notorious people—the very people the Pharisees say are the cause of our troubles. This makes no sense. On top of it, he seems to enjoy wine and good food. If Jesus says the Pharisees' standards are too low, then why would he be lowering himself to associate with these despicable people? And why wouldn't he be less of a partygoer and more of a strict ascetic?

Your curiosity grows. Jesus seems to be a bundle of contradictions. You can't stop wondering about him, trying to figure him out. You get out to hear Jesus every chance you can, and when you can't hear him in person, you ask people you know to summarize his message. Eventually it becomes clear: *this man is not just another revolutionary; he is calling for a revolutionary new sort of revolution.* You've never heard anything like it, and you are both attracted and unsettled.

You turn this over in your mind: Jesus agrees with the violent Zealots and overpious Pharisees (against the status-quo Herodians) that the status quo is wrong and shouldn't be considered acceptable. He agrees with the Pharisees and Herodians (against the Zealots): the solution isn't violent overthrow of the Romans. Yet he disagrees strongly with the Pharisees: you can't scapegoat the prostitutes and drunks and blame them for our problems, but you must instead love them and accept them as God's beloved children. Much about his message is frustratingly unclear and impossible to categorize, but this much is clear: this carpenter's son from Galilee challenges every existing political movement to a radical rethinking and dares everyone to imagine and consider his revolutionary alternative.

What is that alternative? It is to see, seek, receive, and enter a new political and social and spiritual reality he calls the kingdom (or empire) of God, or the kingdom (or empire) of heaven.[4] This kingdom throws down a direct challenge to the supremacy of the empire of Caesar centered in Rome, for in the kingdom of God, the ultimate authority is not Caesar but rather the Creator. And you find your identity—your citizenship—not in Rome but rather in a spiritual realm, in the presence of God (which is what *heaven* means; the idea of chubby angels playing harps on clouds is pop mythology rather than thoughtful theology. More on this in chapter 20).

If you are part of this kingdom, you won't slit Roman throats like the Zealots. Instead, if a Roman soldier backhands you with a blow to the right cheek, you'll turn the other in a kind of nonviolent and transcendent countermove. If a soldier forces you to carry his pack for one mile, you'll carry it a second mile as an expression of your own benevolent free will; you choose a higher option, one above either passive submission or active retaliation. If you are part of this kingdom, you won't curse and damn the notorious sinners and scoundrels to hell; instead, you'll interact with them gently and kindly, refusing to judge, even inviting them to your parties and treating them as neighbors—being less afraid of their polluting influence on you than you are hopeful about your possible healing and ennobling influence on them.

If you're part of this kingdom, you won't be blindly patriotic and compliant like the Herodians and their allies, the Sadducees; instead, you'll be willing to confront injustice, even at the cost of your life. You won't nestle snugly into the status quo, but you'll seek to undermine the way things are to welcome the way things could and should be.

If you're part of this kingdom, you begin to live in a way that some will say is stupid and naive. (Turning the other cheek? Walking the second mile? Defeating violence with forgiveness, sacrifice, and love? Come on! Get real!) But others might see in your way of life the courageous and wild hope that could heal and transform the world.[5]

But how does this revolutionary political agenda fit in with Jewish religion? Is it heretical or traditional, or something beyond both? That's where we must turn next.

CHAPTER 3

THE JEWISH
MESSAGE OF JESUS

He was looking for the kingdom of God.
—LUKE 23:51 ESV

A s I began to realize there is a political and social dimension to Jesus' message I had never seen or been taught, it became clear that in order to better understand Jesus, I needed to take another look at his religious background. I needed to reexamine the Jewish faith in which Jesus came of age, lived, thought, worked, taught, and emerged as an extraordinary prophet.

Although many of us believe Jesus was much more than a prophet, it's certain he was not less. Many Jewish people still argue today, as they did back then, whether he was a legitimate or false prophet. But if we don't see him as a Jewish prophet of some sort, we're not seeing him accurately at all.

Now when we think of prophets today, we tend to think of people who forecast the future or people who start strange new cults or sects. That's not what a prophet was in Jewish tradition.

The best way I've found to understand Jewish prophets is to

see them in dynamic tension with another important religious community in Judaism: the priests. Priests were responsible for the regular, ongoing, day-to-day and year-to-year religious life of Judaism—the key words being *regularity* and its cousin *regulations*. The priests made sure the traditions and practices of regular religious life went on as they should with holidays and sacrifices, feasts and fasts, Scripture and tradition. In Jesus' day, priests were closely allied with the scribes—religious scholars who studied and argued about what exactly the rules and regulations of Judaism should be. Together, they constituted what we might call the religious establishment.

Priests traced their lineage back to Aaron, the first priest and partner of Moses in the liberation of the Jews from Egyptian slavery about 1400 BC. Moses and Aaron also partnered in the birth and development of a post-slavery Jewish identity and culture. Moses was what we might call a revolutionary political leader and liberator, a cross perhaps between George Washington and Nelson Mandela. But he was also known as a prophet, meaning he was someone who heard from God and passed on to the people what he heard—including, notably, a list of commandments that includes the "Big Ten."

There were tensions between Aaron the priest and Moses the prophet, and tensions between priests and prophets continued through the centuries. Priests focused on regularity and tradition, but what happened when people began going through the motions with their bodies, while their hearts and minds were unengaged? What happened when priests had the nation's religious life humming along like a well-oiled machine, but their ritual faithfulness blinded or numbed the people to social injustice or spiritual halfheartedness? In those cases, a prophet would arise and tell the people that God is downright disgusted with external religious observance that rolls along without heartfelt sincer-

ity and without commitment to social justice and practical compassion for the poor and weak.

Consider this passionate—and typical—example from the
prophet Isaiah:

> "The multitude of your sacrifices—what are they to me?" says
> the LORD. "I have more than enough of burnt offerings, of rams
> and the fat of fattened animals; I have no pleasure in the blood
> of bulls and lambs and goats. . . . Stop bringing meaningless
> offerings! Your incense is detestable to me. New Moons,
> Sabbaths and convocations—I cannot bear your evil assem-
> blies. Your New Moon festivals and your appointed feasts my
> soul hates. They have become a burden to me; I am weary of
> bearing them. . . . Stop doing wrong, learn to do right! Seek
> justice, encourage the oppressed. Defend the cause of the
> fatherless, plead the case of the widow." (Isaiah 1:11, 13–14,
> 16–17)

Priests of necessity had credentials: they created and upheld
order, and it was essential that their ordination be orderly—
complete with ordination ceremonies and special religious clothing. They even wore a kind of special cologne (a perfumed oil)
so that they would have a unique scent of holiness.

In contrast, prophets arose without formal credentials or
clothing. The only credential they possessed was a kind of self-
authenticating passion and unavoidable moral substance. As
you'd expect, since their purpose was to disrupt the status quo,
their life and rhetoric were necessarily unruly, disturbing, sometimes shocking. For example, the prophet Hosea scandalized
polite society by marrying a prostitute. The prophet Ezekiel (who
was, like Jeremiah, a bivocational priest/prophet—which made
his wild prophetic behavior all the more shocking) staged a long

public protest in the nude, and on another occasion he staged a public event that involved cooking with excrement. Elijah precipitated a shocking public showdown between himself and a group of pagan prophets who were seducing and misleading the hearts and loyalty of the Jewish people. These and other prophets initiated public spectacles that functioned very much like political demonstrations in modern times: in fact, that's exactly what they were—demonstrations, dramatically embodying in action the message they were proclaiming.

Jesus was not a legitimate priest in the traditional sense. He had no credentials for the Aaronic priesthood.[1] But he was a prophet, arising from obscurity with a shocking, disturbing, unexpected, inflammatory message. And that message was conveyed with prophetic language (hot, fiery, metaphorical, and intentionally jarring) and prophetic action (such as the time he staged a demonstration in the temple—disrupting routines, turning over tables, scattering money, and thus denouncing religious greed, exclusion, and hypocrisy).

Interestingly, in at least four ways Jesus' message of the kingdom of God resonated deeply with themes the prophets had been sounding for centuries. First, like many of the prophets, Jesus spoke on behalf of the poor, the forgotten, the rejected, and the outcasts. In God's kingdom, he said, the last are first. One's status in the kingdom is determined by how one treats little children and "the least of these" (Matthew 5:19). Amazingly, according to Jesus, in the kingdom of God, notorious sinners are loved, welcomed home, forgiven, and reconciled—not rejected. Who is rejected in the kingdom of God? Those who are heartless and merciless toward these often-rejected people!

Second, in strong resonance with the prophetic tradition, Jesus emphasized the inward sincerity of the heart and not mere outward conformity. Outward faithfulness to tradition, he said, can mask inward unfaithfulness toward God. Religious people can become "whitewashed tombs" (Matthew 23:27).

Third, like the prophets before him, Jesus spoke of coming judgment on injustice and hypocrisy. For the ancient prophets, judgment didn't mean that people would be thrown into hell. Rather, it meant that their evil would be exposed and named, and they would suffer consequences of their evil in history, in this life.[2]

But it is the fourth resonance that is especially important: Jesus echoed and intensified the prophetic message that a new world order was possible and coming. The prophets used many images to convey this new world order. They spoke of new heavens, a new earth, and a new heart. They spoke of a day when lions would lie down with lambs (an image not of literal biological upheaval but of social transformation—so that the violent, lionlike people with power would no longer oppress the vulnerable ones: the poor, elderly, orphans, and widows). They described a time when swords and spears would be melted down and recast as farm implements, when nations would not "learn war any more" (Isaiah 2:4 KJV).[3]

I believe that Jesus' message of the kingdom of God becomes especially clear in this fourth context, one which actually includes and combines the other three. A new day is coming—a new earth, a new world order, a new reality, a new realm—in short, a new kingdom. In that new reality, the poor and rejected will be embraced and valued and brought back into the community. In that new era, what will count is what is in the heart—not merely what is projected, pretended, or professed. In that new realm, evil in all its forms will be exposed, named, and dealt with. In that new kingdom, justice, integrity, and peace will overcome.

What's so radical about Jesus' message then? Isn't he just another prophet? Isn't "the kingdom of God" just another prophetic metaphor—and not a wholly original one—for the desired future that critiques and destabilizes the less-than-desirable present?

Here's the scandal: not just that Jesus speaks of the new kingdom (although his image of the kingdom is unique and powerful), but that he says the kingdom is *at hand*, available to be
grasped, knocking at the door—not just someday in the future,
but *here and now*. Here and now!

To a Jewish hearer in Jesus' day, "the kingdom of God" may
have been an accessible and evocative metaphor, but "at hand"
would come as a shock and a contradiction to what everyone
thought. Everyone thought that the kingdom of God could not
happen now; it could only happen then—*later*, after the Romans
were ejected or eliminated, which in turn couldn't happen (for
the Zealots) until *later*, after the Jews were militarily mobilized
and led by a great military liberator (or messiah), which couldn't
happen (for the Pharisees) until *later*, after all the prostitutes and
drunks and other undesirables were either reformed or otherwise
eliminated. Put together, these conditions were so hard to imagine actually occurring anytime soon that they were considered
(by the comfortably adjusted Herodians and their similarly comfortable friends, the Sadducees) completely improbable, no,
practically impossible. The kingdom of God? Maybe in some
distant someday. At hand, here and now? *No way!*

That point of view is very convenient. Think of our reality
today. We might all believe that war and poverty should end
someday, but how many people would believe a self-proclaimed
prophet who arose from, say, Panama or Sierra Leone or Sri Lanka
and was interviewed on CNN or the BBC with this message: "Now
is the time! It's time to decommission weapons programs and reconcile with enemies! It's time for prosperous multinationals to
become rich in generosity! It's time for CEOs to slash their mam-
moth salaries and give generous raises to all their lowest-paid
employees! Don't say 'someday' or 'tomorrow.' The time is today!"
Again, we all might agree that the poor and hungry should be

helped and fed in theory, someday, and perhaps even that the rich should be willing to part with some of their wealth to help make that happen someday. But what if someone arose and said, "The time is at hand! The time is now! Shut down your weapons factories! Open your checkbooks!"

Can you begin to feel the scandal for a prophet to say not, "I'd like to talk to you about the kingdom of God. It's very inspiring to imagine it coming someday" but, "The kingdom of God is at hand!"? Is it hard to imagine why such a prophet—proclaiming peace—would be advised to purchase body armor and a big life insurance policy? The whole "kingdom of God is at hand" project seems to go from bad to worse.

Bad: Jesus' proclamation appears grossly premature and so impractical that it seems completely unrealistic. (Can you see why Jesus would speak so much about having faith that impossible things could happen?)

Worse: Jesus' proclamation threatens the status quo, something that would perhaps appeal to the poor and oppressed, but would inspire something less than enthusiasm among the well-to-do and powerful for whom the status quo was a nice arrangement. (Can you see why Jesus told his followers to anticipate rejection, persecution, and hatred?)

Worst of all: Jesus' proclamation tells the leaders of the nation and the heads of the religious establishment that they have lost their way, forgotten their identity, and proven unfaithful to God. To understand why, we need to dig back even deeper into Jewish identity, back beyond the prophets, back beyond Moses and Aaron, back to Abraham . . . and beyond him, to Adam.

To do this kind of excavation, we have to try to get a high-altitude understanding of the story of humanity from the perspective of Jewish people in Jesus' day, a perspective Jesus himself would have shared.

CHAPTER 4

THE REVOLUTIONARY MESSAGE OF JESUS

Blessed is the coming kingdom of our father David!
—MARK 11:10

In my search to understand Jesus and his message, as I began peeling back the layers of theology and history, seeking to find the core of Jesus' message, I increasingly realized that at the heart of everything there is a story, a deep and grand story. Some might call it a myth, and others might call it factual history. Either way, it is a story that gave meaning and shape to life. It was the story Jesus found himself in. Central to the story are seven characters: God, Adam and Eve, Abraham and Sarah, Moses, and David.[1]

God is the central character in the story right from the moment of creation—"in the beginning" (Genesis 1:1). From the start, God gives creation a fertile goodness, a precious independence, a life of its own, a certain creative freedom—the signature of the good, free, and creative Being who could say, "Let there be light!" and light would be. But creation is never understood as being completely independent of God, for God would always continue to care for creation and interact with it, not from a distance but up close and intimately, not just as an observer but also as a relational participant. In other words, creation would have its own story, but God would always play a role in that story—the role of a good and wise king, with creation as God's domain. (We could call this first episode in the story *Creation.*)

Adam and Eve are the first human characters in the story. Many people today believe that Adam and Eve should be understood as literal historical figures, while others see them as mythic figures whose story has true meaning even if they never actually existed. Either way, they are said to be made "in God's image," which means at the very least that they in a special way reflect the goodness, creativity, and freedom of God (see Genesis 1:27). It is highly possible that "in God's image" actually evokes the idea of God's kingship, with humans having the responsibility to be agents of God's kingship in their care for the earth. Adam and Eve live in a primal human connection to God, an original fellowship and natural friendship with God. But their noble status quickly deteriorates as they disconnect from God and reject any limits placed upon their freedom by their Creator. The results of their disobedience are visible as the story unfolds—a sense of shame and alienation from God and one another, violence of brother against brother, disharmony with creation itself, misunderstanding and conflict among tribes and nations. (This second episode we could call *Crisis.*)

How does God respond to the crisis precipitated by Adam and Eve? Abandon humanity and leave us in the mess we made? Destroy the earth and start all over again? Abrogate our freedom and force us to behave? None of the above. God constitutes a "crisis response team" in the form of a family—a lineage of people who will, through the generations, remember their Creator and their original purpose and who will seek to bring truth, blessing, wisdom, and healing to all people so that God's creation can be rescued from human evil. God begins with an elderly couple, Abraham and Sarah (about 2000 BC), who miraculously conceive in their old age and give birth to the people who will be known as the Jews, people with a special vocation or calling to know God and make God known, to be enlightened and blessed by God, and to enlighten and bless everyone else. (We could call this third episode *Calling*.)

Centuries later, Abraham's descendants have fallen on hard times. They've become oppressed slaves in a world superpower of the day—Egypt; and they have no hope of escape until God calls a man—Moses—to lead them to freedom (about 1400 BC). But how can Moses help Abraham's descendants reclaim their high and holy calling? They have been degraded and humiliated through generations of abuse and slavery; how can they be restored? Moses receives from God and gives to the people the Law or "Torah"—a wise way of living that will shape the people individually and as a community, restoring their dignity so they can rise from slavery's degradation and fulfill their original purpose in the healing of creation. As we've seen, the prophet-leader Moses is joined by Aaron the priest, who will pioneer a priesthood to help the people be instructed and trained as a holy, healthy, and exemplary people. As we've seen, the work of the priests will be supplemented by the prophets and by others (including poets, philosophers, and political leaders) who will carry on a conversation across generations with and about God and about their special relationship—or covenant—with God. (We could entitle this fourth episode in the story *Conversation* or *Covenant*—or perhaps *Conflict*, because remaining faithful to God and God's calling involves great struggle with both internal and external antagonists.)

God faithfully preserves the people of the covenant through many external dangers and internal failures. Finally, they reach a time of stability and peace under the leadership of King David (about 1000 BC). Will they now fulfill their original calling to bring light to all peoples? Sadly, the kingdom of David slowly deteriorates, and two generations later, the kingdom flounders under foolish, arrogant leadership. Civil war ensues, dividing the north and south. Eventually (in 721 BC), the northern descendants of Abraham are ravaged and conquered by Assyria, an expanding empire centered in modern-day Iraq. Then, after a regime change in Iraq, the next regime attacks the southern kingdom and takes their brightest and best to serve in their capital city, Babylon (586 BC). Even after the descendants of Abraham return to their land (in stages, beginning around 537 BC), they remain under the domination of a succession of foreign powers, as we saw earlier: the Persians, the Greeks, and the Romans. The hopes of the people lie in ruins, and the nation is divided into the factions we surveyed in chapter 2.

Imagine Jesus growing up in this story. From his childhood, Jesus has had a sense of special spiritual calling and empowerment—a sense of calling no doubt intensified by his parents, who had reasons of their own for believing Jesus had a historic role to play. How would he understand his world, his times, his life, and his mission? Where would he fit in the story of creation, crisis, calling, and conflict?

From Jesus' first public speech—and *speech* may be too weak a word; *prophetic demonstration* might be more fitting—it is clear that he sees each theme or thread or episode in the story coming together in his time, and he sees his own calling in terms of the heroes we have seen. Luke describes Jesus coming to his hometown, entering the synagogue on the Sabbath, and coming forward to read. He is given the scroll of the prophet Isaiah, and he unrolls the scroll to find a certain passage: "The Spirit of the Lord is on me, because he has anointed me to preach good news to the poor. He has sent me to proclaim freedom for the prisoners and recovery of sight for the blind, to release the oppressed, to proclaim the year of the Lord's favor" (Luke 4:18–19).

Then Jesus dramatically rolls up the scroll, returns it to the attendant, and sits down—sitting being the posture of a teacher in those days. Everyone's eyes are on Jesus, as they wonder what comment he will make on the passage he has chosen. His comment anticipated what he would say about the kingdom being at hand now: "Today this scripture is fulfilled in your hearing" (v. 21).

Jesus seems to see the whole story of his people coming to fulfillment in his time and in his own person. For example, in speaking of the kingdom, he is evoking the memory of David, the great king under whose reign the Jewish people enjoyed unprecedented peace, prosperity, and spiritual vitality. He is claiming to be a new David.

In talking of liberation, he goes back further, evoking the memory of Moses. More, in speaking of a "new commandment" (John 13:34 ESV) or in repeating, "You have heard that it was said . . . But I say to you" (Matthew 5:21–48 NRSV), he is identifying himself as a new Moses, a new lawgiver who gives the people a new law.[2]

In calling people to faith, in choosing twelve disciples, in challenging them to be the light of the world, in sending out his disciples to multiply new disciples of "all nations" (Matthew 28:19), in constantly affirming the need to believe the humanly impossible is possible with God, Jesus returns back further still to Abraham, the man of faith, the origin of the twelve tribes of Israel, the original recipient of the call to be blessed in order to bless "all nations" (Genesis 26:4).

In refusing to draw or respect racial, religious, moral, ethnic, economic, or class barriers, in welcoming non-Jews and treating them with kindness and respect, in eating with both Pharisees and the prostitutes hated by the Pharisees, Jesus shows his primal kinship with all people—a kind of second Adam who seeks to bring people together after so many centuries of distrust and division.

In healing the sick and raising the dead, in performing exorcisms and confronting injustice, in interacting miraculously with the forces of nature, Jesus even identifies himself with the story's original and ultimate hero—God—stating that those who had seen him had in some real way seen God, declaring that he and God were one, and suggesting that through him, God was launching a new world order, a new world, a new creation.

These are not the words and ways of a polite teacher, no matter how brilliant. They go far beyond the claims of a typical priest, poet, or philosopher—and even beyond the bold words of a normal prophet or reformer. These are the primal, disruptive, inspiring, terrifying, shocking, hopeful words and ways of a revolutionary who seeks to overthrow the status quo in nearly every conceivable way. Jesus' words indicate that what has been known as impossible is now becoming not only possible but *actual*.

So, with this background, perhaps we can now picture the Mediterranean world in the time of Jesus. It has been conquered by the most powerful rulers to that point in history: the Caesars. It is centered in history's most powerful and prosperous city: Rome. Its expanding domain, wealth, and military might make it the most powerful empire in all of human history. This political, military, cultural, and economic empire constitutes a status quo that would have reason to think itself "the end of history"—the summit to which all history has been progressing.

Against that backdrop, perhaps we can now imagine an obscure Jewish carpenter without credentials or status, without army or militia or even a weapon, without nobility or wealth, without even

land or a home. With a handful of unimpressive and diverse male
followers and a substantial entourage of supportive women as
well, he travels from village to village, speaking to rustic peasants
and the urban poor, having a special attraction to the unemployed
and the homeless, the disabled and the disadvantaged, the social
outcasts and the marginalized children and women.

Why the poor? Why children? Why the outcasts? Why does
he not only speak to them but also seem to enjoy their company—enjoying their parties, conversing respectfully with them,
and even eating with them, which was a sign of family solidarity
in his day? These—the ones he repeatedly calls "the poor" and
"the little ones" rather than the greatest—are the ones, he says,
who will receive the kingdom of God first.

Why no weapons? Why no well-oiled political machine?
Why live in constant vulnerability? Why not identify a scapegoat, an enemy, a target of hatred? Because, Jesus says again and
again, this kingdom advances with neither violence nor blood-
shed, with neither hatred nor revenge. It is not just another one
of the kingdoms of this world. No, this kingdom advances slowly,
quietly, under the surface—like yeast in dough, like a seed in soil.
It advances with faith: when people believe it is true, it becomes
true. And it advances with reconciling, forgiving love: when
people love strangers and enemies, the kingdom gains ground.

Violent revolutions, in this sense, aren't revolutionary. Noisy
regime changes are utterly predictable—brought about by displays of power and hollow promises and indomitable wealth. In
contrast, the message of Jesus may well be called the most revolutionary of all time:

> The radical revolutionary empire of God is here, advancing by
> reconciliation and peace, expanding by faith, hope, and
> love—beginning with the poorest, the weakest, the meekest,

and the least. It's time to change your thinking. Everything is about to change. It's time for a new way of life. Believe me. Follow me. Believe this good news so you can learn to live by it and be part of the revolution.[3]

This kind of revolution, on the one hand, seems laughable. It's the crazy dream of poets and artists, not the strategy of generals and politicians. Anyone who believes it should be laughed at or perhaps pitied. It's hard to imagine anything more unrealistic— perhaps *pathetic* is the most fitting word for it.

On the other hand, what other kind of revolution could possibly change the world? Perhaps what's crazy is what we're doing and pursuing instead—thinking, after all these millennia, that hate can conquer hate, war cure war, pride overcome pride, violence end violence, revenge stop revenge, and exclusion create cohesion. Perhaps we're the crazy ones!

This revolutionary image of Jesus didn't come to me in Sunday school as a boy. There, Jesus was a nice, quiet, gentle, perhaps somewhat fragile guy on whose lap children liked to sit. Or he was a fellow in strange robes who held a small sheep in one arm and always seemed to have the other raised as if he were hailing a taxi. The revolutionary image of Jesus didn't come to me in adult church either. There, Jesus was someone whose main job was to die so my sins could be forgiven and I could go to heaven (no small thing, of course!), of great value "in my heart" and outside of this world and history, but not terribly important as a public, historical, present factor in relation to the status quo and the powers that be. Or else he was a teacher whose words would be quoted to condemn people our church or denomination didn't approve of. (I'm sad to have to say this; I wish it weren't true.) But Jesus wasn't presented as someone whose message would overturn our thinking as well.

I certainly didn't come across this alternative understanding of Jesus through religious broadcasting. There Jesus seemed to be more of a super-Pharisee, super-Herodian, super-Zealot, or super-Essene rather than a radical alternative to all four. In fact, I had to come to a place of cynically doubting much of what I had been told about Jesus through all these sources so that when I began to read the Bible again, I could see a little more of what I now believe was really there all along. As I did, this revolutionary Jesus began to take shape, and I feel I am still coming to grips with what it means.

Why did it take so long? Why has it been such a struggle? Why didn't anyone tell me all this? Were others trying to hide the truth, or was the truth intentionally hidden by Jesus himself? Is it possible that Jesus was intentionally keeping his message of the kingdom a secret so that it wasn't obvious, wasn't easy to grasp, wasn't like a simple mathematical formula that can quickly be learned and repeated? Is it possible that the message of Jesus was less like an advertising slogan—obvious and loud—and more like a poem whose meaning only comes subtly and quietly to those who read slowly, think long and deeply, and refuse to give up?

CHAPTER 5

THE HIDDEN MESSAGE OF JESUS

You have hidden these things from the wise and learned,
and revealed them to little children.

—MATTHEW 11:25

As you would expect, in my quest to understand the secret message of Jesus, I have read, reread, and reflected on his public presentations. Jesus preached his message of the kingdom of God in public on many occasions over a period of about three years. *Preached* might be a misleading word, though, because to us it's a religious word evoking solemn, well-planned sermons delivered in sacred buildings.

In contrast, Jesus' style wasn't typically religious. His talks often seemed impromptu in response to situations that seemed to arise spontaneously. He might give an entire lecture and never mention God by name—though one got the feeling he was somehow talking about God in his stories of businessmen, fishermen, homemakers, shepherds, dysfunctional families, kingdoms, and farmers. His settings were typically outdoors—on beaches, hillsides, fields, or streets—or in homes. (Whenever he did show up in a religious setting—synagogue or temple—he tended to disrupt the normal proceedings.) The huge crowds that gathered for public proclamations had less the air of a religious service and more the feel of a political rally, or even a festival (Woodstock or Burning Man comes to mind—minus the drugs, sex, and so on).

Jesus' fascinating public communications have indeed given me a feel for the shape and impact of his message, and to those public proclamations we'll turn in the next chapter. But first I must confess that Jesus' private conversations have proved for me equally helpful portals into the message of the kingdom. The four Gospel accounts pulsate with these interpersonal interactions, and each is a treasure waiting to be explored.

Often, Jesus' private conversations arose in consequence to his public proclamations. For example, a man named Nicodemus had heard Jesus teach in public. Intrigued, he then came to Jesus at night to have a private conversation. Why after dark? Probably because Nicodemus was a Pharisee, and being seen with Jesus in broad daylight meant breaking faith with his fellow Pharisees, who by and large hated Jesus.

This conversation unfolds in the third chapter of John's Gospel. Interestingly, John almost never uses the term "kingdom of God" (which is at the heart of Jesus' message for Matthew, Mark, and Luke). There are two exceptions, both of which occur in this unique conversation. Instead, John normally translates "kingdom of God" into another phrase that is notoriously hard to render in English. Most commonly, John's translation of Jesus' original phrase is rendered "eternal life" in English. Unfortunately, the phrase *eternal life* is often misinterpreted to mean "life in heaven after you die"—as are *kingdom of God* and its synonym, *kingdom of heaven*—so I think we need to find a better rendering.

If "eternal life" doesn't mean "life after death," what does it mean? Later in John's Gospel, Jesus reduces the phrase simply to "life," or "life to the full." Near the end of John's account, Jesus makes a particularly fascinating statement in a prayer, and it is as close as we get to a definition: "This is eternal life: that they may know you, the only true God, and Jesus Christ, whom [God has] sent" (John 17:3). So here, "eternal life" means knowing, and knowing means an interactive relationship. In other words, "This is eternal life, to have an interactive relationship with the only true God and with Jesus Christ, his messenger." Interestingly, that's what a kingdom is too: an interactive relationship one has with a king, the king's other subjects, and so on.[1]

The Greek phrase John uses for "eternal life" literally means "life of the ages," as opposed, I think we could say, to "life as people are living it these days." So John's related phrases—*eternal life, life to the full,* and simply *life*—give us a unique angle on what Jesus meant by "kingdom of God": a life that is radically different from the way people are living these days, a life that is full and over-flowing, a higher life that is centered in an interactive relationship with God and with Jesus. Let's render it simply "an extraordinary life to the full centered in a relationship with God." (By the way, I don't expect you to be satisfied with this as a full definition of the kingdom of God. I'm not satisfied with it myself. But it's one angle, one dimension, one facet.)

Now, back to Nicodemus. He comes to Jesus at night and begins with a compliment: "It's obvious you're a great teacher. We're all very impressed with your miracles, which make it clear that God is with you." Jesus doesn't respond with a polite "Thanks for the compliment." Instead, he cuts to the chase and says, "Unless you are born anew, you won't enter the kingdom of God" (see John 3:2–3).

Born anew or *born again,* like *eternal life,* is another frequently misunderstood phrase, one that many people make equivalent to saying a prayer at the end of a booklet or tract, or having an emotional experience at the end of a church service. It often signifies a status achieved through some belief or experience, so that it becomes an adjective: "I'm a born-again Christian." But it's clear that Jesus isn't just talking about a religious experience or status Nicodemus needs to acquire like some sort of certification. No, Jesus is saying, "Nicodemus, you're a Pharisee. You're a respected teacher yourself. But if you are coming to me hoping to experience the extraordinary life to the full I've been teaching about, you are going to have to go back to the very beginning. You're going to have to become like a baby all over again, to unlearn everything you are already so sure of, so you can be retaught."

Nicodemus has only been with Jesus for a matter of seconds, and already he's confused. Why isn't Jesus making his message clear? Why is his message so hidden—in metaphors, in strange and convoluted language? "How can a person be born anew if he's already an adult? This is ridiculous! I'm not supposed to climb back into my mother's uterus, am I?" (see John 3:4).

Something similar happens in the next major episode in John's Gospel, in another conversation—this time with a woman who is only semi-Jewish, belonging to the "half-breed" Samaritans. She's never heard of Jesus before, and she's rather surprised when he, a Jewish man, engages her, a Samaritan woman, in conversation by a well. He asks for a drink, which she gives him. Then he says, "If you knew who I am, you'd ask me for living water" (see John 4:10). *Living water*—an evocative image that sounds like yet another metaphor for "an extraordinary life to the full," yet another metaphor for the kingdom of God. What's that supposed to mean? She's confused. She doesn't know what he's talking about. Why would Jesus be so unclear? Why hide his message in metaphors?

In a story told by Luke, Jesus has a conversation with a man identified as rich, young, and some sort of political official (Luke 18:18–25). He asks Jesus how he can experience "eternal life"— again, not to be confused with "life after you die." He is rich, young, and powerful, yet his life is empty; he's searching for more. Jesus spars with him for a few minutes, questioning the way he has phrased the question. Then Jesus answers his question with a question: "What do you think?" The young ruler gives his answer, and Jesus says, "Good answer. Do that. That will work." The man is confused, because, he says, he's been doing this all his life. Then Jesus gives him a shocking reply: "Liquidate all your wealth, and give it all to the poor. Then come and be my disciple." The man goes away sad, and Jesus is sad as well: you get the feeling he saw real potential in this fellow and liked him a great deal.

In conversation after conversation, then, Jesus resists being clear or direct. There's hardly ever a question that he simply answers; instead, his answer comes in the form of a question, or it turns into a story, or it is full of metaphors that invite more questions. What's going on?

I've asked myself questions like these for years now. I've read and reread the stories. I've consulted commentary after commentary and listened to more than my share of sermons and lectures. Frankly, few experts seem to even notice this pattern of unclarity, of hiddenness, of secrecy—and those who do tend to offer answers that don't ring true, for me anyway.[2]

What could possibly be the benefit of Jesus' hiddenness, intrigue, lack of clarity, metaphor, and answering questions with questions? Why risk being misunderstood—or not understood at all? If the message is so important, why hide it in evocative rather than technical language?

How would you answer those questions? And how do your answers relate to your experience right at this moment, as a person reading this book? And how do they relate to me as I write these words? Am I trying to be clear? Direct? Or hidden? Or a mixture? What difference does it make?

PART 2

ENGAGEMENT:

GRAPPLING WITH THE MEANING
OF JESUS' MESSAGE

CHAPTER 6

THE MEDIUM OF
THE MESSAGE

*The kingdom of heaven may be compared to a man who sowed good seed
. . . a grain of mustard seed . . . leaven that a woman took and hid . . .
treasure hidden . . . a merchant in search of fine pearls . . . a net.*
—MATTHEW 13:24, 31, 33, 44, 45, 47 ESV

I was an English major in college and graduate school. We
English majors spend years learning to do what most people
feel they have learned to do by second grade: *read.* Hopefully the
extra practice helps us reach a reading level at least a little above
average. When I read the teachings of Jesus with my English-
major sensitivities, I can't help but notice this: the heart of Jesus'
teaching comes to us in a unique literary genre known as *parable.*

Parables are to Jesus what jokes are to a comedian. Matthew
13:34 makes the point through grand hyperbole (an English-major
term meaning an intentional exaggeration used to convey truth):
"He did not say anything to them without using a parable." Why
would Jesus do this? Why would he indulge in an art form—a
short fictional narrative—to convey his essential message?

The best introduction to parables—if by introduction you
mean "getting thrown into the deep end of the pool so you can

learn to swim"—is found in Matthew 13, with a parallel in Luke 8. In this passage (I'm hoping you'll read it on your own, right now, before proceeding), Jesus tells a succession of parables that have several fascinating commonalities.

First, each parable ends with a repeated phrase (English majors might call this a refrain): "Whoever has ears to hear, let him hear." That phrase is almost a parable in and of itself. What could Jesus mean by it? *Don't just listen with your ears; listen with your heart. Don't just hear my words; hear my deeper meaning. Don't listen for the literal meaning accessible to your rational mind; seek deeper for a meaning that requires that you make a personal investment of your sincere effort and your imagination.* (Do Nicodemus and the Samaritan woman from the previous chapter come back to mind?) *Don't think I'm just talking about literal, physical birth or water; realize I'm talking about something much deeper.*

Second, each parable involves a hiddenness that eventually becomes visible. As we read Matthew 13, we are presented with one image after another of this hidden-to-visible pattern. We have generic *seeds* planted in a generic field—seeds in which are hidden the potential of a mature plant and eventually a harvest of thousands more seeds, seeds that are hidden in soil where their germination and growth are mysterious and concealed until they sprout and mature. We have *weeds*, whose identity is initially hidden because they resemble grain, secretly planted—again, where they can't be seen—among grain until their identity is made manifest at harvesttime. We have a *mustard seed* planted—hidden under soil—whose potential for growth eventually becomes clear. We have *yeast* kneaded—or hidden—in a lump of dough, where it rises mysteriously and visibly transforms the dough. Similarly, we have *treasure* hidden in a field, an exceptional *pearl* hidden among average pearls, a mix of edible and inedible *fish* caught in a net—fish themselves being hidden under water until they're caught in the net, and their identity as good or useless being hidden until they are removed from water and sorted. The pattern, though understated, is powerfully conveyed through this repetition.

Third, each parable involves surprise—a surprising variety of harvests, a surprising infestation with weeds, a surprising answer about what to do about the weeds, a surprising size of the full-grown mustard plant, and so on.

Even without reflecting on each parable for the unique and specific insights it yields, perhaps we can begin to get some idea of how parables work. They hide the truth so that we need to do more than simply "hear with our ears" or "read with our eyes" on a literal level; we have to invest ourselves in an imaginative search for meaning—a meaning that will surprise us when we discover (dis-cover or unhide) it for ourselves.

This is exactly what happens in Matthew's account. The disciples hear Jesus tell the first parable, but they can't figure it out on their own—they have ears, but they can't hear, to use Jesus' own language. So they come back to Jesus with a fascinating question—the same question we're asking here, actually: "Why do you speak to the people in parables?"

One might expect the disciples to ask, "What does this parable mean?" But instead they ask *why*: "Jesus, why are you doing this? You're telling these stories, but nobody is getting your point. Can't you find a clearer, more direct, obvious approach?"

Parables entice their hearers into new territory. If the goal is an interactive relationship (which is at the heart of terms like *kingdom of God* and *eternal life*, as we have seen), a parable succeeds where easy answers and obvious explanations couldn't. With a clear and easy explanation, hearers can listen and achieve understanding and then go on their way, independent of the teacher. But when a parable confounds them, it invites them to ask questions, so they continue to depend on the teacher himself, not just their independent understanding of his words.

So if a parable leaves you confused, you will have one of two responses. You can respond with arrogant and impatient anger ("I have no idea what he's saying. This is a waste of time!"), which makes you walk away. Or you can respond with eager and curious humility ("I can't let this go. I must know more!"), which keeps you coming back. In this way parables have a capacity that goes beyond *informing* their hearers; parables also have the power to help *transform* them into interactive, interdependent, humble, inquisitive, and persistent people.

In Matthew's narrative, Jesus' response is as fascinating as the disciples' question. He explains that they are being given a great gift: "the knowledge of the secrets of the kingdom" (13:11). He goes on to explain, quoting the ancient prophet Isaiah, that when people's hearts become calloused, they lose their ability to see and hear at deeper levels. In other words, the crowds may hear Jesus' words with their physical ears, but they miss the message that can only be heard by the heart—as "whoever has ears to hear, let him hear" suggests.

Maybe then, we have some beginning of an answer to the disciples' question, and ours. Why did Jesus speak in parables? Why was he subtle, indirect, and secretive? Because his message wasn't merely aimed at conveying information. It sought to precipitate something more important: the spiritual transformation of the hearers. The form of a parable helps to shape a heart that is willing to enter an ongoing, interactive, persistent relationship of trust in the teacher. It beckons the hearer to explore new territory. It helps form a heart that is humble enough to admit it doesn't already understand and is thirsty enough to ask questions. In other words, a parable renders its hearers not as experts, not as know-it-alls, not as scholars . . . but as children.

Now do some of the most famous sayings of Jesus begin to make more sense—about the kingdom of God belonging to children, about needing to become like a little child to enter the kingdom, about needing to be born again? Children are dependent, not independent. They can't learn unless they ask questions of people they trust. Their thirst for knowledge expresses itself in an unquenchable curiosity, a passionate inquisitiveness.

This, by the way, is what the problematic word *repentance* is all about. The word means to rethink—to reconsider your direction and consider a new one, to admit that you might be wrong, to give your life a second thought, to think about your thinking. It means, just as Jesus said to Nicodemus that night, that you have to begin again, become like a child again, be born again. So if the problem is that too many of us are too independent, too self-centered, too set on stubbornly sticking to our own self-determined path . . . if the problem is that too many of us are arrogant know-it-alls, closed-minded adults, overconfident non-thinkers, and altogether too grown up—then the parable renders us into exactly what we need to be: teachable children. No wonder Jesus decides to make his message a secret! No wonder he hides it in metaphor and story!

But not all of us are willing to be so rendered. Some of us want fast, painless, effortless information and not slow, energetic, engaging transformation, thank you very much. What happens then to those who say, "I don't have time for childish stories about seeds and yeast and sheep. I'm an important person. I have advanced degrees! I'm very knowledgeable!"? Simply put, the parable excludes them. In fact, the parable exposes them. In that sense, while parables bring some to childlike, humble rethinking, they bring out the arrogance, anger, impatience, and ugliness of others.

When I first began to understand that this was part of what was going on in Matthew 13, I felt bad. I didn't want anyone to be left out. I didn't want anyone to be exposed. Couldn't Jesus' parables be 100 percent effective? Couldn't there be a happy ending for everybody? Couldn't they get through to everybody? (More on this in chapter 18.)

In Jesus' story, the answer was either no or not yet, because many, many people didn't respond as the disciples did to Jesus' parables. They didn't ask questions, they didn't soften their hearts in a childlike way, and they didn't seek "the secrets of the kingdom." Others did get the message, but it didn't win their hearts; it made them angry! Once, for example, Jesus told a detailed parable about some people who resorted to horrific violence to maintain control over their little turf. The religious leaders who felt their turf being threatened by Jesus got the meaning and hated it because, according to Luke, "they knew he had spoken this parable against them" (20:19). Their response was to become more dedicated to their own hostile schemes.

We might wish Jesus' parables could have won over even the Pharisees. (A few, by the way, *were* won over—including Nicodemus, Joseph of Arimathea, and later, a Pharisee named Saul, better known to us as Paul, who became a leading apostle in the early Christian movement.) But if it's the heart that counts, then hearts can't be coerced; nobody can be forced. They can be invited, attracted, intrigued, enticed, and challenged—but not forced. And that, perhaps, is the greatest genius of a parable: it doesn't grab you by the lapels and scream in your face, "Repent, you vile sinner! Turn or burn!" Rather, it works gently, subtly, indirectly. It respects your dignity. It doesn't batter you into submission but leaves you free to discover and choose for yourself.

Maybe that's why the message of the kingdom of God comes, then, not as a simple formula or list of information and not as an angry threat or ultimatum, but instead as a secret hidden in a parable, like a treasure hidden in a field, like a seed hidden in soil, like yeast hidden in dough.

Human kingdoms advance by force and violence with falling bombs and flying bullets, but God's kingdom advances by stories, fictions, tales that are easily ignored and easily misunderstood. Perhaps that's the only way it can be.[1]

CHAPTER 7

THE DEMONSTRATION
OF THE MESSAGE

*Heal the sick . . . and say to them, "The kingdom
of God has come near to you."*
—LUKE 10:9 ESV

L et's suppose a TV news reporter walked up to Jesus and said,
"Jesus, we have thirty seconds before the commercial break.
Can you tell us in a sentence or two what your message is about?"
What would he say?

"Everyone needs to rethink their lives as individuals, and we
need to rethink our direction as a culture and imagine an
unimagined future for our world," he might say. "Because the
kingdom of God is here. You can count on this."

The reporter might say, "Er, well, yes. And how exactly would
you define the kingdom of God? We have fifteen seconds."

I can imagine Jesus saying, "Well, the kingdom of God is like
a man who had two sons . . . " A few sentences into the story, the
reporter interrupts and cuts to the commercial break. Jesus just
blew his chance to turn his message into a sound bite. Off cam-
era, the reporter is curious: "Would you finish the story about the

man with the sons?" Jesus tells the story and prepares to leave. But the reporter, still curious, suggests they get a cup of coffee. They go into a coffee shop, and the conversation continues: "Let me ask you again—could you define this thing you call the kingdom of God?"

Jesus begins, "It's like a woman who was making bread."

"No," the reporter interrupts, "I don't want to know what it's *like*. I want to know what it *is!*"

Jesus smiles and says, "Well, the kingdom of God is like a coffee merchant seeking the best fair-trade, organically grown beans . . ."

Did Jesus communicate the message of the kingdom of God in any way other than secretly through parables? The answer is no, if you limit yourself to words. But the answer, beyond words, is yes; he also communicated the message secretly through signs and wonders.

The term we typically use for these phenomena is not *signs and wonders* but rather *miracles*. Yet too often these days, the word *miracle* unwittingly roots us in a worldview that is foreign to the world of Jesus. To understand how miracles worked as vehicles for Jesus' secret message, I think we're wiser to immerse ourselves in Jesus' worldview rather than drag him into ours.

A worldview is a way of seeing. It's not just what we see, but how we see everything else. It's the lens through which we see—a lens of assumptions, beliefs, images, metaphors, values, and ideas that we inherit and construct from our family, our teachers, our peers, our community, and our culture. As we go through life, many of us find it next to impossible even to *want* to question our inherited worldview, while others do exactly that: we rethink, we imagine other ways of seeing things, and we sometimes experience radical conversions out of one worldview and into another.

Most of us in the modern West—religious or irreligious—
have inherited a worldview that was formed largely in the seven-
teenth century. In this perspective, our world is best compared to a
machine. God, if God exists, created the universe like a huge clock:
the complex mechanism was designed and wound up in the beginning, was set in motion, and has been ticking away ever since,
slowly winding down through a process called entropy. Or it could
be compared to brightly colored billiard balls racked up on a green
felt table: in the beginning, God arranged the table and hit the
white cue ball, and ever since, balls have been bouncing into balls
as the universe unfolds in a closed chain of cause and effect.

In this worldview, miracles—if they occur—would involve
interference from outside. God reaches in and fiddles with the
gears of the clock, or God intervenes and pushes a billiard ball so
its natural path is redirected. In this view, God is the outsider; natural causes create effects mechanically and automatically unless
God intervenes. Some people believe God does intervene, overcoming the natural mechanisms. They are often called super-
naturalists. Others believe either that there is no God or that the
God who exists would never intervene, cheat the rules set up at
the beginning, introduce any new causes into the system, or inhibit
any effects. They are often called naturalists (or reductionists).

But Jesus lived long before clocks, billiard tables, or complex
machines of any kind. His worldview, his model of the universe,
was very different—more organic, less mechanistic. In many
ways it was simpler, but in many ways it was grander, more alive,
freer, subtler, and more dynamic: God was neither absent and
outside the universe nor trapped inside it. Rather, God was connected to the universe, present with it, and intimately involved
in it. So the universe was less like a machine and more like a family, less like a mechanism and more like a community. The very
word *kingdom* suggests as much: kings are relationally involved in

their kingdoms. They are present, active, participatory, and engaged. They aren't simply a part of the kingdom—one part among many—but neither are they apart from it.

The balance here is quite rich and multidimensional. On the one hand, kings are not absent, disengaged, distant, and presently uninvolved like a machine engineer who designed and built a clock and now has left to let it run on its own, or like a pool shark who after taking his shot steps back from the table, leans against the wall, smokes a cigarette, and lets things happen from a distance. On the other hand, kings are not, strictly speaking, in absolute control. They don't control their kingdom the way a kid playing a video game operates the controls of the game, for example. No, in this more nuanced and organic worldview, kings have an interactive relationship rather than either uninvolved distance or intrusive control; they have real power and authority, but that power and authority are used among citizens who also have wills of their own. The king may give orders, but the citizens may disobey. The king may make laws, but the citizens may ignore them. Then the king may respond to their incivility and so on, in an ongoing interactive relationship.

So for ancient Jews the universe was not a simple, controlled, mechanistic system. It was a complex, organic community with both limits and freedom, accountability and responsibility. It had room for freedom both for God and for humanity. There were limits, and there was order—but there were also breathing room and real possibilities to choose and make a life. In this universe, God gives us space and time to live our lives. We have a measure of freedom, but our freedom doesn't eradicate God's freedom. God has freedom, but God's freedom doesn't extinguish ours. As we've said before, it's a universe in interactive relationship with God. (In this light, Jesus' invitation into the kingdom of God was an invitation into the original universe, as it was meant to be.)

In order to understand what Jesus' signs and wonders meant, then, we need to try to expand beyond our modern, Western, naturalistic, mechanistic, reductionistic universe and make ourselves at home in this larger and more relational universe. We will understand neither signs and wonders in particular nor the idea of the kingdom of God in general if we try to shrink them into our restrictive universe. We have to meet these phenomena in their natural habitat.

As we've already seen, the ancient Jews understood humanity to have been plunged into crisis because we humans have abused our freedom. We steal, kill, and destroy. We hoard, rape, and plunder. We oppress, victimize, lie, and cheat. We undervalue precious things and overvalue worthless things. As a result, the whole organism or community of the world has become sick, and its sickness is ugly, painful, and terminal, adversely affecting every woman, man, girl, and boy.

Let's go back to our imaginary reporter—who, in spite of being a teller of stories, continues to resist Jesus' stories. "Excuse me, Jesus, I'm sorry to interrupt. Some other time I may be interested in hearing more of your stories. But isn't there a way you can tell me about the kingdom of God other than st—" The reporter begins coughing and can't finish the sentence. "I'm sorry. It's these cigarettes," she says, pointing to a box in her purse. "I've been a chain smoker for years, and lately I've wondered if I've got lung can—" Another round of violent coughing follows.

Imagine that Jesus leans across the table and touches her on the arm. "Would you like to be healed of that cough?" he asks.

"I'd like to be healed of my nicotine addiction while I'm at it," she says with a laugh—and another round of coughing.

"That can be arranged," Jesus asks. "Do you believe God can heal you?"

Suddenly the reporter grows serious. "I do, I suppose, believe it's, you know, theoretically *possible*. But my faith is so microscopic," she replies.

Jesus says, "It only takes a microscopic amount of faith, like this grain of sugar here on the table. So your microscopic faith has healed you." The reporter suddenly realizes that the urge to cough and the impulse to smoke are both completely gone. She takes a breath and realizes her lungs haven't felt so full and healthy in years. "There's a breath of the kingdom of God," Jesus says. With a smile, he gets up, drops some money on the table, and walks out of the coffee shop.

The reporter gets up and chases him out the door. "What just happened to me? What's going on?"

Jesus stops on the sidewalk, looks back at the reporter, and says, "This was a sign, a wonder. As a sign, it *signifies* the reality and nature of the kingdom. As a wonder, it fills you with *wonderment*. It makes you think. It breaks all of your categories of what is possible and impossible. That's how the kingdom is. What is impossible with humanity is possible with God."

Although there is no shortage of fool's gold in our world, still I do believe in the real gold of signs and wonders.[1] I firmly believe that God is interactive, engaged, alive, and participating in our world, and I believe that we experience—sometimes often and sometimes seldom, sometimes dramatically and sometimes subtly—touches of God's grace.[2] These experiences are *significant*—they are signs to us of God and God's activity. And they are *wonderful*—they make us wonder what's going on and fill us with wonder. They are by nature inexplicable. They confound our attempts to account for them through mechanisms, causes, or formulas, and so they help liberate us from the tyranny of the impossible.

What do I mean by the tyranny of the impossible? When I was a boy growing up in the United States, racism was everywhere.

(It still is, I know, in subtler but still-too-real forms.) If you had talked about a day when people could enjoy genuine harmony with their neighbors and be enriched by their racial differences, people would have said, "Impossible!" In South Africa, the overt system of apartheid made hope for racial reconciliation seem even more impossible.[3] When everyone "knows" something is impossible, nobody even attempts it. Why waste their time? But look at what's happened in recent decades: what was impossible has become—if not yet fully real—at least truly possible.

A woman with a drug addiction, a man with a rage problem, a country torn by religious strife, a religious community racked with internal conflict, a school with chronic underachievement, a growing gap between rich and poor, a carbon-based economy radically out of sync with the natural environment—all of these can appear to be intractable, stubborn problems and earn the label "impossible to change." But when the kingdom of God comes near, when we experience it, the word *impossible* deconstructs. It melts and evaporates, and its tyranny over us ends.

These kinds of impossible experiences accompanied Jesus almost everywhere he went. (I say *almost everywhere* because there were some places—see Mark 6:5, for example—where people were so locked in their worldview that they couldn't experience anything that would open it up to signs and wonders, even in the presence of Jesus.) Some signs and wonders were dramatic and public, such as when thousands were fed with a few morsels of food, when a storm was suddenly calmed, or when a dead person was brought back to life in the middle of a funeral procession. Others were less public and more personal, such as when a heartbroken mother and father got their little girl back from death or when a Roman soldier's beloved household servant was cured.

Each sign and wonder was creative and unique, refusing to be reduced to a formula or mechanism. For example, once Jesus cured an illness with spit and mud, another time by washing in water, another by coming close and touching the sick person, and another time simply by saying a word from a distance. Yet in spite of their diversity, it is possible to make a few generalizations about Jesus' signs and wonders.

First, they involve healing rather than destruction. Jesus doesn't call down fire on resistant people and destroy them. (In fact, he sternly rebukes his disciples for even mentioning such a thing.) He doesn't make his critics fall to the ground, writhing in pain. He doesn't blind an army so they can be defeated. He doesn't cause floods that drown his antagonists. Rather, his miracles invariably bring healing—with one exception, in which a fruitless tree was killed and used as a sign and wonder of a different type.

Second, they are related to faith. The relationship is complex, because sometimes Jesus' miracles occur in response to faith and at other times they occur in order to stimulate faith. Interestingly, Jesus often minimizes his own role in the process by saying, "Your faith has made you well" not, "I have made you well" (see, for example, Luke 8:48; 17:19; 18:42). But Jesus sometimes emphasizes his role, as when he heals a paralyzed man with these words: "So that you may know that I have power on earth to forgive sins . . ." (see Matthew 9:6). Even here, though, the healing demonstrates something visible—healing a body—so that people will have faith that Jesus can do something invisible—forgiving sins. So signs and wonders can stimulate faith, and they come in response to faith. They seem to be part of an ascending spiral of growing faith.[4]

Third, as we've seen, signs and wonders have a symbolic or secret meaning. We've already considered Jesus' language of "having ears to hear" with the heart, so it seems natural that his healing of deafness would signify helping people hear the truth in their heart. Healing blindness would suggest helping people "see the light." Healing paralysis would symbolize helping people, religions, and cultures get moving again so they can be fruitful and creative once more. And what could be a more powerful dramatization of the possibility of a new beginning than raising the dead? What might calming a storm signify, or feeding thousands with a boy's sack lunch (with seven or twelve baskets of crumbs left over), or curing an embarrassing "female problem" like a chronic menstrual disorder, or liberating someone from seizures and self-destructive behavior?

Fourth, Jesus generally tells people to be quiet about signs and wonders. You would think that miracles would be the greatest marketing method ever invented, so Jesus would tell people to spread the word. Some have wondered whether telling people to keep quiet about their experience was a kind of reverse psychology intended to promote this very thing. But I think that Jesus' "don't tell" policy was more related to his overall strategy with his secret message—a strategy of understatement, hiddenness, and quietness: better to have something brewing, bubbling, fomenting under the surface than to have more sizzle than steak. (Jesus may also have simply wanted to avoid the unmanageable crowds that would have resulted from highly promoted signs and wonders![5])

Fifth, it's clear that Jesus' signs and wonders aren't in themselves the point. Rather, like road signs, they point to the point. Tourist traps and public-relations stunts draw attention to themselves, but signs point to something beyond themselves—a destination or a path or something worth noticing. What do they point to?

Let me answer that with a kind of parable of my own. If you get a glimpse of soldiers in camouflage uniforms sneaking through the forest, if you notice planes from an enemy country flying high above you, if key political leaders in your country disappear or are mysteriously assassinated, you might suspect that an invasion is coming. If bullets start flying and bomb sirens start going off, your suspicions will be fulfilled. Another nation—let's call it a kingdom—is preparing to invade and conquer your kingdom.

But what if this kingdom that is invading is a kingdom of a very different sort? What if the invasion is one of kindness and compassion rather than force and aggression? What if sick people start getting well suddenly and inexplicably? What if rumors spread of storms being calmed, insane people becoming sane again, hungry people being fed, and dead people rising? Couldn't this be the sign of a different kind of invasion—the coming of a different kind of kingdom?

That's how I have come to understand the signs and wonders of Jesus. They are dramatic enactments of his message; they are the message of the kingdom spread in media beyond words. They combine to signify that the impossible is about to become possible: the kingdom of God—with its peace, healing, sanity, empowerment, and freedom—is available to all, here and now. Signs and wonders unbolt the mechanisms that tell us what is mathematically and practically possible and impossible. They make way for faith that something new, unprecedented, and previously impossible is on the move. They tell us we are being invaded by a force of hope, a group of undercover agents plotting goodness.

Some scholars see the stories of signs and wonders as fictions—parables, if you will, composed by the early church. Although I respect their differing viewpoint, I am not among them. I believe that signs and wonders actually, factually clustered around Jesus and his secret message of the kingdom of God—just as we might expect if Jesus and his message were truly from God. But I don't believe they occurred in the way of a billiard player reaching in to flick a few balls on the table with his finger. Rather, I have become convinced that Jesus' worldview is better than ours. It's not that an external intruder is fiddling with the laws of nature. It's not that the mechanism is being tampered with from the outside. Rather, it's that the universe isn't a machine at all; it's more like a family, a community, or a *kingdom*. And God isn't positioned outside of the universe, reaching in occasionally, but rather God is here, in it with us, present, near.

In fact, this is in large part what I believe the signs and wonders of Jesus are secretly telling us: that God, the good King, is present—working from the inside. The King is in the kingdom, and the kingdom is among us here and now—for those who have eyes to see and ears to hear. The King is present in the mess and chaos of everyday life on earth, bringing healing, sight, perception, liberation, wholeness, wholesomeness, movement, health, fullness, nourishment, sanity, and balance. The incursion of the kingdom of God has begun. We are under a gentle, compassionate assault by a kingdom of peace and healing and forgiveness and life.

Could Jesus' secret message become any clearer than that?

CHAPTER 8

THE SCANDAL
OF THE MESSAGE

*If it is by the finger of God that I cast out demons,
then the kingdom of God has come upon you.*
—LUKE 11:20 ESV

As the story of Jesus unfolds, as his secret message grows clearer and brighter, the background drama paradoxically turns tense and dark, foggy and ugly: Jesus' enemies are out to get him, and he isn't being careful. Instead, he climbs out on a limb and hands them a saw, in parable teasing them, in overt statement taunting them, in public demonstration inviting them to retaliate, in provocative statement tempting them to misinterpret.

Take, for example, the events of what we call Palm Sunday, five days before Jesus' crucifixion on Good Friday: the "triumphal entry" into Jerusalem when a crowd treats Jesus as a king and the religious leaders tell him to stop them but he refuses, or the "cleansing of the temple" when Jesus disrupts temple protocols, or his telling the religious leaders that little children understand more than they do. He is intent, it seems, on goading his enemies from disgust to fury, from fury to scheming, from scheming to outright violence: "Woe to you, scribes and Pharisees! The prostitutes will enter the kingdom before you do! You strain out gnats and swallow camels! You're like whitewashed tombs! You clean the outside of the cup, but the inside is full of rot and stench! Woe to you!"

Why does Jesus do this? Is he some sort of loose cannon, a hothead who can't control his rhetoric? Or is there a secret method to his apparent madness?

What if the secret message of Jesus requires a secret method? What if standard politics, standard communication tactics, standard promotion and marketing and molding of public opinion won't work for a secret message like his? What if Jesus' unprecedented message requires a method so unusual as to be scandalous?

In the previous chapter, you may have noticed that I strategically avoided an important issue. Among the many signs and wonders of Jesus, I never mentioned one of the most important and—to many of us—strangest: Jesus' confrontations with evil powers. Those demonic confrontations give us a window, I believe, into Jesus' secret method to bring his secret message to fruition.

The language of demons and devils seems to many people outdated and primitive, mythical and superstitious. Does one have to believe in a literal devil and demons in order to understand Jesus and his message? Or is it possible for us to read the exorcism stories with a kind of intentional naiveté, suspending judgment long enough to see what insight may come if we don't dismiss them or explain them away too quickly? That's what I recommend for those who are unable to honestly accept satanic imagery as factual: suspend judgment long enough to see what insight appears after taking the stories at face value.

If we leave questions of factuality suspended, in the end I believe we will agree on this conclusion: for Jesus' secret message of the kingdom to be realized, it must first expose the evil of all alternative kingdoms or regimes or systems or ideologies. And for that evil to be exposed, it must be drawn out of the shadows, where it hides in secret.

On the level of demonic confrontations, this drawing out into the light happens again and again. A child is thrown into suicidal convulsions. Jesus arrives and draws out the invisible evil spirit that causes the child to behave in this visibly bizarre and heartbreaking way—and the boy is healed. A man lives among tombs, cutting himself, refusing to wear clothing. Jesus arrives and draws out the unseen evil spirits that cause this seen behavior—and soon the man sits clothed and in his right mind. Thousands come to Jesus with various afflictions and internal oppressions, and Jesus draws into the light whatever oppressive, destructive, disease-causing, imbalancing, paralyzing, or convulsing forces hide within them so they can be freed and restored to balance and health. This liberation and restoration become—as we saw in the last chapter—visible signs of Jesus' secret message. At one point, he says plainly and stunningly, "If I drive out demons by the finger of God, then the kingdom of God has come to you" (Luke 11:20).

That might be the whole story: the kingdom has come through Jesus, liberating and healing individuals from oppressive spiritual powers. But what if this individual strategy is itself a sign pointing toward Jesus' larger strategy—for the nation and perhaps the world? What if it is yet another sign and wonder pointing to his larger, less obvious strategy: to draw corporate or even cosmic evil out from the shadows and into the broad daylight, so that it can be seen and named and rejected and banished?

What do I mean by corporate and cosmic evil? We've all heard terms like *team spirit* or *school spirit*, the *soul of a nation* or *corporate culture*, the *crowd mentality* or *feeding frenzy*—terms that express how a kind of groupthink can emerge in a group and then take it over, "possess" it, drive it. We've all heard stories or had experiences in which people were caught up in an evil "spirit"—often expressed in terms ending in -ism, such as Nazism or terrorism. What if, beyond referring to the possession of individuals by evil spirits, the demonic gives us language to personify and identify these covert forces that enter groups of us, using us, becoming a guiding part of us, possessing and influencing and even controlling us—dirty, ugly, sick, but unrecognized motivations and drives that take us places we never would have gone otherwise?

What has become most striking to me about Jesus' confrontations with demonic powers is this: individual evil spirits may be behind the scenes (whispering through Jesus' disciple Peter or putting thoughts of betrayal into Judas Iscariot's mind), but by and large, Jesus deals with them pretty straightforwardly. His dominant opposition arises not from dirty personal demons crouching in darkness but rather from dirty systems of power and violence operating in powerful people who function in broad daylight. Just as he draws out and drives out hidden demonic invaders, Jesus must draw out, expose, name, reject, and banish this systemic, transpersonal evil—incognito beneath robes and crowns, hiding in temples and palaces, camouflaged behind political slogans and images on coins, covert in policies and traditions, seeming to "possess" groups so they think and move in an awful choreography. Jesus' signs and wonders of demonic deliverance seem to signify that very real and dangerous forces of evil lurk and work in our world—as common in groups as the demonic torments of disease and insanity are in individuals. This transpersonal evil can possess, oppress, sicken, and drive insane whole nations, religions, and other social networks just as personal demonic spirits possess, oppress, paralyze, and convulse individuals.

Again and again, Jesus seeks to lure covert systemic evil out of the shadows and into the light where it can be named, exposed, and expelled. He does so in a number of ways. Sometimes he directly confronts it—such as when he goes into the temple and turns over the money changers' tables, when he calls the religious leaders hypocrites and wolves disguised as sheep, or when he intentionally and publicly heals someone on the Sabbath, inviting the fury of the religious elite. Their violent and hateful reactions show their true character and confirm Jesus' assessment of them. Sometimes he makes ambiguous statements, easily misunderstood, exposing his neck, so to speak, to those who will take the chance to slit it—such as when he said the temple would be destroyed and he would rebuild it in three days. His critics interpret his statements in the worst possible light and again, in their ugly response, show what they're made of and what drives them.

By drawing out covert evil so that it manifests itself, Jesus exposes the dangerous "spirits" that can inhabit the most respected of institutions—*government* (the Roman Empire, Herod's puppet kingdom), *political movements* (Zealots and Herodians), *religious parties* (Pharisees and Sadducees), *religious structures and hierarchies* (chief priests), *professions* (scribes), and *family systems* ("Do not call anyone on earth 'father'" and "let the dead bury their own dead," Jesus says of these systems [Matthew 23:9; 8:22]). Perhaps most striking of all, he shows that evil can invade even *Jesus' own band of disciples,* and it can do so at the least expected moments. For example, Satan enters Judas, we are told, while he sits at what we call the Last Supper (John 13:27). And no less significant: Jesus says to his lead disciple, Peter, "Get behind me, Satan!" immediately after Peter has been the first to correctly identify Jesus' true identity (Matthew 16:23). In each case, Jesus names the evil among his own followers.[1] What could these unexpected incursions and exposures of evil mean? What do they teach us?

Jesus' confrontations with demonic forces draw us right back to his secret message: a new force, a new spirit is in the world—not a demonic spirit, but the Holy Spirit. Just as sick, destructive spirits can take possession of groups, this new Spirit is entering people and forming them into a healthy, creative, and new kind of community or society—the kingdom of God. This kingdom represents a counterforce, a countermovement, a counterkingdom that will confront all corrupt human regimes, exposing them, naming them, and showing them for what they really are. The new kingdom—unlike its evil counterparts—doesn't force itself where it is not wanted and welcomed. For all its power and reality, it comes subtly, gently, and secretly.[2]

Interestingly, Paul, a second-generation leader in the movement started by Jesus, commonly speaks of realities that sound very much like this corporate way of seeing the demonic.[3] He speaks of diverse regimes—thrones and dominions, principalities and powers—language that serves as a kind of shattered mirror image of Jesus' cohesive language of the one *kingdom of God*. These forces of evil, in Paul's mind, are not simply invisible, individual devils hiding in between neurons in individuals. Instead, they are very real and powerful forces that enter groups of people and guide or even control their internal functioning and external behavior. Under their influence, people move together as with one will, like a school of tuna or a flock of crows or a herd of wildebeest, paralyzed or convulsed or twisted or massaged so as to conform to values and dictates that they may never have imagined on their own.[4]

In the drama of Jesus' life, two of these invisible but real transpersonal forces in particular are exposed as opposing God's kingdom. First, Jesus confronts the Roman Empire, which many Jews identify as the source or focal point of all evil and trouble among them. Ironically, reading the narratives of Jesus' life, one is struck not by the strength of the Roman regime but rather by its weakness. A Roman centurion—a representative of the empire—comes to Jesus, seeking healing for a beloved household servant. For all his power to control and destroy with swords and spears, he can't indulge his compassion in his own home and needs a greater power to heal. This greater power he recognizes in Jesus. Even in the climactic trial scenes late in the Gospels, Rome's puppet governor Pilate seems like a skittish petty politician, not a frightening potentate. He's manipulated by crowds, pressured by his wife, conflicted and paralyzed internally, fearful of making a decision until he is forced to do so, and even then he appears far from resolute and confident. Jesus stands before him, flogged and beaten, mocked and bound, waiting for Pilate to pass judgment. Why at that moment does Pilate seem the insecure one, asking, "What is truth?" and why does Jesus seem at peace, powerful in his refusal to answer questions—keeping the truth, as it were, to himself—confident that Pilate's power is insignificant, that Pilate can do nothing unless the power is given him by another source? It's a striking scene—a sign and wonder, if you will.

In the face of the simple moral authority of Jesus, the power and authority of Rome seem brutally grotesque and ethically pathetic. One thinks of the Chinese students standing down tanks in Tiananmen Square in 1989, or Nelson Mandela ascending from prison to the presidency in South Africa in 1994, or Martin Luther King Jr. sitting in prison in Birmingham in 1963—exercising greater moral leadership while under arrest than the prison guards, police forces, and governors who thought they were in control. One thinks of the Catholic prayer protests that exposed the weakness of Communism in Poland, or the weaponless crowds toppling Communism in Romania, or Gandhi—not an identified Christian, but one who seemed to understand the secret way of Jesus better than many Christians—as he led nonviolent resistance against imperialism and religious hatred. Jesus' message of the kingdom of God scandalizes by showing the weakness of the apparently powerful and the power of the apparently weak.[5]

Second, Jesus confronts the equally dark spirit of the religious elite of his day. It is one thing to show the weakness of the apparently powerful; it is another to show the evil of the apparently righteous. And this is what Jesus does. Step by step, he draws them out. He dances on their dividing lines, violates their taboos, honors their villains, and vilifies their honorees. He tells the truth to them, inviting their fury. Their blood pressure rises and their pulses pound; their brows and palms go sweaty; their jaws and fists clench and unclench until their elegant robes can no longer hide the true desires, values, fury, and rage seething beneath their folds. When Pilate presents Jesus to the crowds, beaten and bloody, they shout, "Crucify him!" And even more scandalous, they declare, "We have no king but Caesar!" Faced with the kingdom of God, they choose the kingdom of Caesar.

These religious leaders (like so many today) have pretended to be about religious piety and national fidelity. They seemed to want liberation from Caesar. But now they manifest their true desire: to affiliate with the powers that be, to maintain sovereignty in their little turf and the continuation of their little religious regime, as if to say, "May *our* will be done!" If Jesus' secret message threatens their domain, they will scream for Caesar to bolster their leverage. Their true colors—pale, bilious, gangrenous—have shown through.

The story is familiar: the religious and political-military powers collaborate and negotiate and reach an elegant final solution: Jesus will be crucified as a rebel. He will be nailed to a Roman cross—the visible symbol of the power of the Roman principality and power, the instrument of torture and execution that is the end of all who stand up against Rome.

They crush him and his movement. And it appears that Jesus has failed.

This is the scandal of the message of Jesus. The kingdom of God does fail. It is weak. It is crushed. When its message of love, peace, justice, and truth meets the principalities and powers of government and religion armed with spears and swords and crosses, they unleash their hate, force, manipulation, and propaganda. Like those defenseless students standing before tanks and machine guns in Tiananmen Square, the resistance movement known as the kingdom of God is crushed.

But what is the alternative? We really must consider this question. Could the kingdom of God come with bigger weapons, sharper swords, more clever political organizing? Could the kingdom of God be a matter of what is often called *redemptive violence?* Or would that methodology corrupt the kingdom of God so it would stop being "of God" at all and instead become just another earthly (and perhaps in some sense demonic) principality or power? Perhaps the kingdom could come with flawless, relentless, irresistible logic—a juggernaut of steamroller counterarguments to flatten every objection. Or would that mental conquest be as dominating as military conquest, reducing the kingdom of God to a kingdom of coercive stridency?

What if the only way for the kingdom of God to come in its true form—as a kingdom "not of this world"—is through weakness and vulnerability, sacrifice and love?[6] What if it can conquer only by first being conquered? What if being conquered is absolutely necessary to expose the brutal violence and dark oppression of these principalities and powers, these human ideologies and counterkingdoms—so they, having been exposed, can be seen for what they are and freely rejected, making room for the new and better kingdom? What if the kingdom of God must in these ways fail in order to succeed?

Perhaps at this moment, we are getting a brief and fragmentary glimpse into one of the deepest mysteries of the kingdom of God. In this light, perhaps the death and resurrection of Jesus shimmer as the most profound sign and wonder of all, showing the scandalous truth that no human system can be trusted, that all -isms are potentially demonic and idolatrous "graven ideologies." Perhaps this understanding of the kingdom reveals the horrible truth that even church and state with their sacred theologies and ideologies, like all other structures of this world, will—given the chance—execute God so they can run their own petty kingdoms.[7] What if our only hope lies in this impossible paradox: the only way the kingdom of God can be strong in a truly liberating way is through a scandalous, noncoercive kind of weakness; the only way it can be powerful is through astonishing vulnerability; the only way it can live is by dying; the only way it can succeed is by failing?

Can you see why such a message is too subversive to be overt? Can you see why it must be kept—no, not kept but rather told—as a secret? Can you see why the people on top (the powerful go-getters, hee-hawing in the thrill of success and power) would have no interest in such a secret, subversive, scandalous message, and why those who are underprivileged (the poor, mourning, excluded, and meek) would in a sense occupy a privileged position for "getting it"?

Looking back on Jesus and his message, Paul spoke of the Cross as the weakness and foolishness of God (1 Corinthians 1:18–25). But that weakness and foolishness, he said, were more powerful than the wisdom and power of humanity with all its ideology, methodology, religiosity, ingenuity, and violence. When Paul looked at the Cross, he saw that "God was reconciling the world to himself in Christ, not counting people's sins against them" (2 Corinthians 5:19 TNIV). Somehow, for him, the defeat of Christ on that Roman cross—the moment when God appears weak and foolish, outsmarted as it were by human evil—provided the means by which God exposed and judged the evil of empire and religion, and in them, the evil of every individual human being, so that humanity could be forgiven and reconciled to God. And the reconciling movement resonating out from Christ's life, teaching, death, and resurrection is what we mean by the kingdom of God.

This understanding of the secret message of Jesus makes sense of a number of odd details of the gospel story, such as why the resurrection of Jesus wouldn't be miraculously broadcasted to millions as irrefutable evidence of Jesus' legitimacy. Can you see it? As soon as the evidence becomes irrefutable, it takes on a kind of domineering power—the kind of force so effectively yielded by principalities and powers. Instead, in keeping with the kingdom of God's secret, paradoxical, and apparently weak power, the first in on the secret are a few women—unacceptable in their day as legitimate witnesses in court—vunerable people who can easily be ignored and dismissed by those who prefer the status quo, the powers that be, the systems and regimes that function as "kingdoms of this world." These humble women will be believed only by those who want to believe, those who freely choose to believe.

What an inefficient system, you might be thinking. *Surely there must be a better plan.*

If you can think of a better plan, let the rest of us know, and you may just become the savior of the world. But before you reject this plan, you'd better be sure yours is truly better. This one has no peer that I have ever encountered or been able to imagine.

CHAPTER 9

YOU CAN'T KEEP A SECRET

This gospel of the kingdom will be preached in the whole world as a testimony to all nations.

—MATTHEW 24:14

The four Gospel accounts differ in many ways—emphasis, language, which events are included and not included—but they share a common conclusion: after the death and resurrection of Jesus, Jesus sends his disciples into the world with a mission. Let's look at each version:

- *Matthew:* "Go and make disciples of all nations, baptizing them in the name of the Father and of the Son and of the Holy Spirit, and teaching them to obey everything I have commanded you" (28:19–20).
- *Mark:* "Go into all the world and preach the good news to all creation" (16:15).
- *Luke/Acts:* "Stay in the city until you have been clothed with power from on high." . . . "You will receive power when the Holy Spirit comes on you, and you will be

my witnesses in Jerusalem, and in all Judea and Samaria, and to the ends of the earth" (Luke 24:49; Acts 1:8).
- *John:* "As the Father has sent me, I am sending you" (20:21).

Assuming that each of the Gospel writers is giving us either different wordings of the same commissioning or different instances of a general commissioning that was uttered in various ways on multiple occasions, we can integrate the four versions like this:

> You can't keep the secret of the kingdom to yourselves. I am now sending you, as the Father sent me, to communicate the good news of the kingdom of God. Those who receive your message, you should form into learning communities of practicing disciples so they learn to live according to my secret message, just as you are learning. You should not do this in your own power, but you must rely on the power of the Holy Spirit. And you shouldn't stop at the borders of your own culture, language, or religion, but you must cross every border and boundary to share with all people everywhere the secret you've learned from me—the way, the truth, the life you've experienced walking with me.

That last proviso—that the disciples spread their message globally—was more radical than we may realize. First of all, among the polytheists who constituted the majority of the ancient world, there were many gods who had territorial legitimacy. It was quite novel to proclaim one universal God, not restricted to one language, culture, religion, or region—and especially to do so without seeking to spread its native political regime and culture along with it. But more surprising, Judaism—

even though it believed in one universal God—was typically not a missionary religion, so Jesus' global commissioning of his disciples is especially surprising. Judaism's preoccupations, as we have seen, were its own internal affairs—gaining political liberation from Roman occupation or, if not that, calming internal tensions between various factions, avoiding trouble with the Romans, and setting its national religious and moral life in order.

Yet this idea of global mission was in another sense not unprecedented. As we mentioned in chapter 4, the primal calling of the primal Jew, Abraham, had implicit global dimensions: "I will bless you and make you a great nation, and *all nations* of the world will be blessed through you" (see Genesis 12:2–3). The resonance between those words and Jesus' commission to "make disciples of *all nations*" is unmistakable. But the ancient Jews, like their more recent monotheistic colleagues, often devolved into being preoccupied with being blessed themselves, forgetting or suppressing their calling to be a blessing to others. They, too, often saw their calling as *exclusive* ("We are blessed to the exclusion of all other nations") rather than *instrumental* ("We are blessed for the benefit of all other nations").

The prophets and poets who arose unpredictably through Jewish history frequently reminded the people of their global calling and rebuked them for their parochial exclusivism.[1] Even with the words of the prophets in their national consciousness, though, the people may well have thought, *Perhaps we will be a blessing to other nations someday—but that won't happen until we are free from foreign occupiers.* Jesus seems to say, "The kingdom of God doesn't need to wait until something else happens. No, it is available and among you now. So start spreading the blessing spoken of by Abraham now. Invite people of all nations, races, classes, and religions to participate in this network of dynamic, interactive relationships with God and all God's creation! I've taught you how to live in the kingdom way; now it's time for you to teach others. Go on! Get going now!"

And that is what they did. Luke's second document in the New Testament, the Acts of the Apostles, tells their story, and Jesus' secret message of the kingdom is their theme from beginning to end. Luke reports that Jesus "presented himself alive after his suffering by many proofs, appearing to them during forty days and speaking about the kingdom of God" (1:3 ESV). The disciples speak of the kingdom throughout the book of Acts, beginning with Philip, who "preached good news about the kingdom of God and the name of Jesus Christ" (8:12 ESV).

The apostle Paul continued in the same tradition in his extensive travels, "strengthening the souls of the disciples, encouraging them to continue in the faith, and saying that through many tribulations we must enter the kingdom of God" (14:22 ESV). Later, in Ephesus, Paul "entered the synagogue and for three months spoke boldly, reasoning and persuading them about the kingdom of God" (19:8 ESV). He characterized his entire ministry as "preaching the kingdom" (20:25), and Luke's memoir ends like this: "[People] came to [Paul] at his lodging in great numbers. From morning until evening he explained the matter to them, testifying to the kingdom of God and trying to convince them about Jesus . . . proclaiming the kingdom of God and teaching about the Lord Jesus Christ with all boldness and without hindrance" (28:23, 31 NRSV).

I had an experience many years back that helped me conceive of this commissioning, given by Jesus and played out in the book of Acts. It was a rather quiet afternoon, and I was working in my office, preparing a sermon or something similar. The phone rang. "Hello, is this Brian McLaren? Do you recognize my voice?" The voice was deep, but I didn't recognize it. "My name is Stephen Crabb," he said, but I still didn't know who he was. "I have a son named Scott."

Then it clicked. I said, "Scott Crabb—he was a camper at a summer camp where I worked back when I was in college."

"Yes," the deep voice replied. "He's my son. You taught him something. Do you remember what it was?"

I did. "As I recall, I taught him how to play four or five chords on the guitar—C, F, G, and A minor. I remember him having a lot of trouble with F."

"Yes, that's why I'm calling," he replied. "You told my son something else."

"I used to tell people if they really want to learn to play, buy a guitar but don't ever put it in the case. Leave it out, and they're more likely to pick it up and play it when they sit in front of the television or whatever," I said.

"Yes, and Scott did exactly what you said," Mr. Crabb told me. "Scott went on to major in classical guitar in college. In fact, he received a master's degree in guitar performance. During his studies, Master Segovia heard him play and invited him to be one of his last students. You know, Master Segovia was already very old and frail at the time and knew that he would not be taking on more students after this group."

A smile spread across my face. To think that a teenager I had helped become interested in the guitar had gone on to become a student of the greatest classical guitarist ever! But Mr. Crabb wasn't finished. "Well, last week, my son had his master recital. Master Segovia was there. As you can imagine, I was deeply proud, and I thought back over the years and remembered you. I decided to look you up and tell you that one of your students went far. You got Master Crabb started in his profession." Then he said thanks and good-bye, and I never heard from him again. I never even got a chance to say thanks for calling.

I remember sitting in my office as two feelings struck me. First, I felt great joy that I had had the honor of influencing Scott in this direction. And second, I felt a curiosity: I don't think I had ever heard the word *master* said so frequently in such a short time—*Master* Segovia, *master* recital, *Master* Crabb. I thought of other uses of the word—master craftsman, for example. And then it hit me: this is what Jesus did with his disciples.

Jesus was master of making the music of life—not just with wood and string, tuners and frets, but with skin and bone, smile and laughter, shout and whisper, time and space, food and drink. He invited the disciples to learn to make beautiful life-music in his secret, revolutionary kingdom-of-God way. He helped each of them learn the disciplines and skill of living in the kingdom of God. They watched him play, watched him live and interact, and imitated his example until they began to have the spirit of his style, the power of his performance. Then, after his resurrection, he said, "This was your master recital—living through the agony of my rejection, humiliation, crucifixion, burial, and resurrection. Now you are ready to be sent out as masters yourselves—masters of my secret message, masters in living life in the kingdom."

Master musicians do three things. First, they continue to practice their craft. If they don't continue to practice, they'll get rusty and nobody will be interested in their work. I'm sure that no master teacher would allow her student to progress to the master recital unless she was confident the student would indeed continue to practice so as to be worthy of the title master musician himself or herself. Second, master musicians perform. They play! They bring the joy of music to audiences everywhere. And third, they are authorized to take on students themselves.

So Jesus called twelve students or apprentices—which is what *disciples* means—and demonstrated the art of living in the kingdom of God. He gave them three years of private lessons, if you will. Now, eleven of them have passed the tests necessary to be sent out as master artists and teachers—or *apostles*—themselves. Called together to learn and practice, sent out to practice, play, and teach—that is the life of a disciple and apostle, and that's what Jesus' commissions his band of disciples to be and do around the world.

The whole kingdom-of-God project, then, began as a community of people learning to love and play the music of the kingdom in the tradition of the Master and his original apprentices. The story of the kingdom is the story of this band of life-musicians over the last two thousand years. From parent to child, mentor to mentoree, teacher to student, friend to friend— the art of living, performing, and teaching in the kingdom of God has been passed down through centuries and passed on across continents. Often their music has been sweet and beautiful, but—we must admit this—too often it has also been ugly, out of tune, unworthy of the Master composer and musician they claim to follow. Often, after an especially bad season of disappointing performance when the art of the kingdom is nearly lost, a new master musician will arise and reinfuse the tradition with vitality and passion—a St. Patrick, a St. Francis, a Teresa of Avila, a Hildegard of Bingen, a John Wesley, a C. S. Lewis, a Desmond Tutu, a Mother Teresa. Many of us feel that the Christian tradition today is in need of some new artists who have the music of the kingdom deep in their souls to revive the tradition in our world, especially in the West.

Sadly, for centuries at a time in too many places to count, the Christian religion has downplayed, misconstrued, or forgotten the secret message of Jesus entirely. Instead of being about the kingdom of God coming to earth, the Christian religion has too often become preoccupied with abandoning or escaping the earth and going to heaven. Too often its members have forgotten the teachings of Jesus about making peace and turning the other cheek and crossing boundaries to serve people formerly considered "outsiders." We have instead launched or baptized wars, perpetuated racism, and defended an unjust status quo. We have betrayed the message that the kingdom of God is available for all, beginning with the least and the last and the lost—and have instead believed and taught that the kingdom of God is available for the elite, beginning with the correct and the clean and the powerful. We have been preoccupied with guilt and money, power and fear, control and status—not with service and love, justice and mercy, humility and hope. Frankly, our music has too often been shallow, discordant, or played with a wooden concern for technical correctness but without feeling and passion. Or it has been played with passion but has departed from the true notes, rhythm, and harmonies of the Master. And whenever that happens, our audiences do exactly as they should: they ignore us and our message, or they turn from us in boredom or disgust.

Jesus himself said this would occur. He anticipated that his followers would cool in their passion and drift from his message. He warned them not to hide their light under a bucket or lose their saltiness; if they did, they would be "trampled under foot" (Matthew 5:13 NRSV). He promised them that if they simply mouthed the right words without actually living the way of the kingdom of God, if they were like trees full of leaves but not fruitful in deed, if they stopped loving one another but instead became judgmental or callous or greedy for money and power, their faith would be worthless and people would know they were frauds. Church history—including recent church history—has proven Jesus right in these predictions.

In my work and travels, I see too much of this religious bombast: busy, chatty, manic, or monotone religion without the heart of Jesus' message of the kingdom of God. But thankfully, I also see that wherever the secret message of Jesus is believed, pro-claimed, and lived, transformation occurs—transformation of individuals, faith communities, neighborhoods, and even cultures.

When this quiet transformation is happening, when things are going right, people often hardly notice; after all, as Jesus said, the kingdom advances as subtly as a seed growing or as yeast ris-ing in a loaf of bread. But when they do notice, there's the un-mistakable sense that God is present, and people can't help but breathe out prayers of thanksgiving to God. In spite of our many failures, the secret is getting out!

CHAPTER 10

SECRET AGENTS OF THE SECRET KINGDOM

Truly, I say to you, the tax collectors and the prostitutes go into the
kingdom of God before you. . . . Therefore I tell you, the kingdom of God
will be taken away from you and given to a people producing its fruits.
—MATTHEW 21:31, 43 ESV

It was the most religious who seemed to get the secret message of Jesus the least, and the least religious who seemed to
get it the most. True, the religious could make a contribution;
Jesus said that every religious scholar "who has been trained for
the kingdom of heaven is like a master of a house, who brings
out of his treasure what is new and what is old" (Matthew 13:52
ESV). But even so, *kingdom* is not a particularly religious word,
and Jesus seemed to go out of his way to describe the kingdom
in ways that common people could understand. Kingdoms may
have priests and preachers, but they also must have farmers, governors, painters, engineers, drivers, writers, carpenters, scientists,
diplomats, teachers, doctors, nurses, cooks, philosophers, sculp-
tors, and even lawyers.

Too often, when the story of the movement of Jesus is told,
most of the focus is on the religious professionals. But what if

their role is at best minor? What if the real difference is made in the world not by us preachers but by those who endure our preaching, those who quietly live out the secret message of the kingdom of God in their daily, workaday lives in the laboratory, classroom, office, cockpit, parliament, kitchen, market, factory, and neighborhood?

There's a beautiful glimpse of this outworking of the kingdom of God in one of the New Testament documents, Paul's letter to Titus. There, he tells slaves—who made up a large percentage of Roman society—that they have a role to play in the kingdom of God. Beautify the message about God our Savior, he tells them, by your way of life, by your integrity as you do your daily work (Titus 2:10). Now this subtle outworking of the kingdom of God works in at least two ways. First, it gives slaves an unheard-of dignity in their current status. Second, over time, that dignity will begin to undo the very institution of slavery itself.

The same thing happens with teachers, politicians, lawyers, engineers, and salespeople who take seriously their identity as participants in the kingdom of God. The way they teach, the way they develop public policies, the way they seek justice, the way they design and work with resources from God's creation, the way they buy and sell—all of these are given dignity in the context of God's kingdom, and soon, transformation begins to happen. After all, when you see your students, constituency, clients, or customers as people who are loved by God and as your fellow citizens in God's kingdom, it becomes harder to rip them off or give them second best. And when enough people begin to live with that viewpoint, in little ways as well as big ones, over long periods of time, things truly change. Education as we know it evolves, as do public policy, law, manufacture, and economics. In this way, each of us not only prays, "May your kingdom come," but we also become part of the answer to that prayer in our sphere of influence.

So now, perhaps, the dimensions of the secret message of Jesus become clearer and clearer. Jesus forms a movement of people who trust him and believe his message. They believe that they don't have to wait for this or that to happen, but rather that they can begin living in a new and better way now, a way of life Jesus conveys by the pregnant phrase *kingdom of God*. Life for them now is about an interactive relationship—reconciled to God, reconciled to one another—and so they see their entire lives as an opportunity to make the beautiful music of God's kingdom so that more and more people will be drawn into it, and so that the world will be changed by their growing influence. Everyone can have a role in this expanding kingdom—women and men, masters and servants, powerful and powerless, old and young, urban and rural, white collar and blue collar, previously religious and previously irreligious. Each life can add beauty to the secret message of Jesus. Each person can be a secret agent of the secret kingdom.

This idea—that the kingdom of God is about our daily lives, about our way of life—may lie behind the tension people feel between the words *religious* and *spiritual*. Perhaps the word *religious* has come for some people to mean "believing in God but not the kingdom of God." And perhaps the word *spiritual* has become a way for others to mean "living in an interactive relationship with God and others as a daily way of life." In this way, the influence of Jesus may be as strong outside of some religious institutions as inside— and maybe even stronger. This may even help explain why church attendance has been plummeting across Europe and in many parts of the United States. When Christianity sees itself more as a belief system or set of rituals for the select few and less as a way of daily life available to all, it loses the "magic" of the kingdom.

I've spent a lot of time in Europe during the last ten years or so. I love to visit the beautiful cathedrals in whatever city I visit. I often will sit quietly and feel the gentle grandeur of their past. Before long, though, I also feel the poignant pathos of their present, since many of them attract tens or hundreds of times more tourists than worshipers in an average week.

What went wrong in those cathedrals? And what is going wrong in much of the stagnant, tense, or hyped-up religiosity of churches in my own country? Those questions take us beyond the scope of this book, but you can guess one of my main hunches: the Christian religion continues to sing and preach and teach about Jesus, but in too many places (not all!) it has largely forgotten, misunderstood, or become distracted from Jesus' secret message. When we drifted from understanding and living out his essential secret message of the kingdom, we became like flavorless salt or a blown-out lightbulb—so boring that people just walked away. We may have talked about going to heaven after we die, but not about God's will being done on earth before we die. We may have pressured people to be moral and good or correct and orthodox to avoid hell after death, but we didn't inspire them with the possibility of becoming beautiful and fruitful to heal the earth in this life. We may have instructed them about how to be a good Baptist, Presbyterian, Catholic, or Methodist on Sunday, but we didn't train, challenge, and inspire them to live out the kingdom of God in their jobs, neighborhoods, families, schools, and societies between Sundays.

We may have tried to make people "nice"—quiet citizens of their earthly kingdoms and energetic consumers in their earthly economies—but we didn't fire them up and inspire them to invest and sacrifice their time, intelligence, money, and energy in the revolutionary cause of the kingdom of God. No, too often, Karl Marx was right: we used religion as a drug so we could tolerate the abysmal conditions of a world that is not the kingdom of God. Religion became our tranquilizer so we wouldn't be so upset about injustice. Our religiosity thus aided and abetted people in power who wanted nothing more than to conserve and preserve the unjust status quo that was so profitable and comfortable for them.

What would happen, I wonder as I sit in the light of the glorious stained-glass windows of a cathedral in Prague or Vienna or London or Florence, if we again tasted the good news of Jesus—not as a tranquilizer but as vibrant, potent new wine that filled us with joy and hope that a better world is possible? What if, intoxicated by this new wine, we threw off our inhibitions and actually began acting as if the hidden but real kingdom of God was at hand?

I sit in those great cathedrals and grieve this terrible loss of identity and direction, this sad adventure in missing the point. It may sound strange to say, but I feel sorry for Jesus, sorry for the way we've dumbed down, domesticated, regimented, or even ruined what he started. But inevitably I also begin to imagine the secret message of Jesus being explored and explained and celebrated in those cathedrals once again, and I can imagine standing-room-only crowds filling those sacred spaces in the not-too-distant future. Back home, I can imagine kids and young adults not dropping out of churches (as they so often do when our churches are purveyors of bad or mediocre news), but instead bringing all their friends so they, too, can share in the secret message, the truly good news of the kingdom of God. I can imagine us abandoning the bad idea that some people are "clergy" (the special ones who perform) and others are "laity" (the passive ones who observe—and often critique—the performance of the clergy). Instead, I can imagine us seeing everyone as potential agents of the kingdom.

So how do you become a secret agent of the kingdom of God? For example, let's say you own a company that manufactures computers. Your job is to discover how your computer company can align and participate in the kingdom of God. In other words, your company could help fulfill God's will—or it could frustrate and oppose God's will being done on earth and specifically in the computer industry. You work each day not just for a paycheck but also for the kingdom of God to come more and more fully in your company and through it. You seek to lead your company in such a way that your employees and clients can get a taste of God's kingdom in the fairness, diligence, integrity, teamwork, respect, pride, and fun they experience at your company. Computer people can work in God's kingdom.

Or let's say you're a soccer mom. You live in the suburbs, drive a minivan, bake cupcakes for the second-grade class, volunteer in an English tutoring program for new immigrants, and try to make it to aerobics class at least once a week—or more likely, once a month. You increasingly see yourself as an agent of the kingdom of God among the young soccer players and their families, and among your neighbors in your elementary school district, with the immigrants who become not only your students but also your friends, and with your exercise partners who sweat together at the health club. The idea of being an agent of God's kingdom infuses your imagination with new possibilities for your life. What if you, sometime next year, organized a stream cleanup that educated the people in your neighborhood about the local watershed, which is, after all, your address in God's creation? Then the year after that, what if you organized a project at your elementary school to raise money for an orphanage in Burundi, a project that not only helped orphans but taught your child and her classmates that they have neighbors whose lives are very different from their own—and that we are all bound together as neighbors in God's kingdom? Then the year after that . . . Do you get the point? Soccer moms can participate in God's kingdom.

Maybe you're a lawyer. You can seek justice and serve your clients as an agent of God's kingdom. Maybe you're a reception- ist. You can make your office a hospitable place and welcome people in a way that makes them feel that God's kingdom is real and present. Maybe you're a state governor or corporate consult- ant or rock star or police officer or military officer. All of these jobs can become vocations if you engage in them as an agent of God's kingdom.

Maybe you think you have the most boring, degrading, and unfulfilling job in the world. What would happen if you saw your job as one component—large or small, enjoyable or depressing— of your larger, deeper, grander calling as a participant in the kingdom of God? Would it change your attitude?

Consider this true story about a man I just met. Carter is about seventy-five years old, African-American, and a taxi driver in Washington, D.C., where I live. He's been driving a taxi for years. A few weeks ago, he picked up my friend Don, and they became friends. Don and I were working on a project to draw attention to the genocide in Darfur, Sudan, and Don invited Carter to come to one of our events. Don introduced us there, and Carter told me his story.

Back in 1994, Carter served as taxi driver for a man from Malawi, Africa. Because Carter wasn't "just a taxi driver" but instead was "a taxi driver in the kingdom of God," he treated his guest with special respect as only a taxi driver in the kingdom of God can. The guest introduced Carter to some other Malawian friends, and soon Carter the taxi driver was invited to visit Malawi, which he did, in 1998.

There, Carter saw poverty he had never before imagined. He

prayed, "Lord, help me bring some joy to this village." And God answered his prayer. First, Carter realized that there was no road in the village—just a narrow path, rutted and muddy. (This is the kind of thing a taxi driver would notice. If I had been there, I would have noticed they needed a library.) With a proper road, people could get around better, and elderly and sick people could be transported to the hospital. He had brought some money, so he offered to pay for gas and oil and drivers if the people of the village would do the work. Soon Carter's generous spirit—the spirit of the kingdom of God—became contagious, and someone provided a grader and then more and more people volunteered to help. Three days later, they had built a proper road a mile and a quarter long.

A year or so later, he returned to the village. A young man had been falsely accused of stealing and was stuck in jail. Since Carter seeks the kingdom and justice of God wherever he goes, he got involved, and soon the young man was set free. On this same visit, Carter met a boy who needed medical care that was available only in a distant city. Carter made it possible for the boy to get treatment on a regular basis by finding and convincing—who else?—a driver to take him.

The next year, he went back again and this time helped some young men improve their farming. (Carter is not an agricultural-ist, but he used money he had saved from his job as a taxi driver for the kingdom of God to buy them some additional seeds.) He made connections and got twenty-six soccer balls donated to the children of the village, because in the kingdom of God, fun and play are important things. Carter knew this. He even helped them get uniforms, because in the kingdom of God, dignity and pride are also important things.

On another trip, Carter the taxi driver's generosity inspired a shopkeeper in the village to donate money to help some sick children get treatment for ringworm. Soon a Bible school was launched, and it grew from seventeen to eighty-five students quickly. No wonder—when you see signs of the kingdom of God coming to your village, you would want to learn all you can about it!

Roads, rides, seeds, ringworm medicine, soccer balls and uniforms, a Bible school—these are all signs of the kingdom of God in that little village. Carter told me, "I don't do any of this myself. God is doing it through me."

Carter is a taxi driver in Washington, D.C. He's also a secret agent in the kingdom of God. There are thousands of Carters out there, millions. They aren't on TV. They aren't on the radio. Nobody has ever heard of them. They don't write books. They don't need to, because their days are pages in the most important book of all.

THE OPEN SECRET

If a kingdom is divided against itself,
that kingdom cannot stand.
—Mark 3:24

However good we judge the secret message of Jesus to be, as we've seen, we have to face the fact that the career of the Christian church too often compares unfavorably. I speak as a person who loves the church and has devoted my adult life to serving it, so I speak with sadness. But I also speak the truth. Why is there such a difference? Some theologians and scholars have concluded that—rightly or wrongly—the message of the Christian church became a different message entirely from the message of Jesus.

I was having lunch one day with a well-known scholar and writer when this contrast hit me in the face. We were eating in a Chinese restaurant in Tyson's Corner, Virginia. I was sipping my hot-and-sour soup when he said, "You know, most evangelicals haven't the foggiest notion of what the gospel really is." I considered myself an evangelical, so I felt a bit challenged by his statement. In response, I stared at my soup, hoping he'd resolve the issue without asking my opinion; but he was too good an educator for that. "What would you say the gospel is, Brian?"

I answered by quoting the apostle Paul in the New Testament—statements about justification by grace through faith, the free gift of salvation, Christ being a substitutionary sacrifice for my sin. "That's exactly what most evangelicals say," he replied, letting the tension hang for what seemed to me like a long, long time. I looked up from my soup and asked, a little defensively, "Well, then, what would you say the gospel is, if it's not that?" I was preparing myself for heresy, not for enlightenment, since I was quite confident in my quotations from Paul.

"The kingdom of God is at hand. That was Jesus' message. Don't you think we should let Jesus tell us what the gospel is?" His reply confounded me. Of course I had to agree with him. But I could see no connection between the message of the kingdom of God and the gospel as I understood it from Paul.

How did I deal with the tension? I didn't. Somehow, I just put it aside. I sat on it. I ignored it. It was several years later, when I began the quest that led to the writing of this book, that "the hot-and-sour soup conversation" came back to me.

Few topics are hotter and more sour than this among theologians today. Some would say that we have exchanged "Christianity" for "Paulianity." Christianity was about the kingdom of God coming to earth for everyone, they would say. Paulianity is about a select few escaping earth and going to heaven after they die. They would see Paul as the enemy who ruined the good thing begun by Jesus. However, I don't think Paul is the enemy; I think our misinterpretations of Paul are the enemy. I think Paul is actually a friend of the gospel of the kingdom, perhaps its best friend since Jesus. But you shouldn't agree with me until you consider the data.

First, the language of the kingdom is more common in Paul's letters than many realize. If you were to do a search for the word *kingdom* in the writings normally attributed to Paul, you'd find just over a dozen references.

On four occasions, he speaks about "inheriting the kingdom of God," and in each case, he does so to specify what kinds of behaviors will disqualify people from inheriting it: sexual immorality, greed, drunkenness, idolatry, envy, and so on (1 Corinthians 6:9, 10; Galatians 5:21; Ephesians 5:5). In one other instance, he says that "flesh and blood cannot inherit the kingdom of God" (1 Corinthians 15:50), apparently referring to the experience of resurrection after death.[1]

In two instances, he describes what the kingdom of God does not presently consist of ("food and drink" in Romans 14:17 NRSV and "talk" in 1 Corinthians 4:20) and what it does consist of ("righteousness and peace and joy in the Holy Spirit" in the first passage and "power" in the second).

In two instances, Paul again refers to the kingdom of God as an already-present reality, and in two others as a reality for which people presently work and suffer:

1. The Colossian believers have been transferred from "the domain of darkness" to "the kingdom of [God's] beloved Son" (Colossians 1:13 ESV).
2. The Thessalonian believers have been called into God's "own kingdom and glory" (1 Thessalonians 2:12 NRSV).
3. Paul's colleagues are described as "fellow workers for the kingdom of God" (Colossians 4:11).
4. The Thessalonian believers are proving themselves worthy of the kingdom of God as they endure suffering for it (2 Thessalonians 1:5).

In three final instances, Paul seems to lean more toward a future or coming reality of the kingdom of God:

1. He anticipates "the end, when [Christ] delivers the kingdom to God the Father after destroying every rule and every authority and power" (1 Corinthians 15:24 ESV).
2. Paul charges an apprentice leader "by [Christ's] appearing and his kingdom" (2 Timothy 4:1).
3. God will rescue Paul from evil plots and save him "for his heavenly kingdom" (2 Timothy 4:18 NRSV).

The Christianity versus Paulianity argument undervalues those thirteen overt references to the message of the kingdom. (We will return to the future dimension of the kingdom of God in chapter 19.) It also seems to miss an insight that can be made clear through a few simple analogies.

If Albert Einstein was effective as a physicist in the early twentieth century, the next generation of physicists doesn't simply repeat his experiments and confirm them ad infinitum, but instead they build on his work and extend it into new territory. New questions are raised, and new problems are presented by his new theories; the next generation shows their confidence in Einstein's discoveries not by talking about them constantly but by attending to those new questions and problems. They may hardly ever say $E = MC^2$. They may write little of general relativity. But this isn't necessarily a rejection of Einstein's work; it could mean the logical extension of his work into new territory.

Or if Dr. Martin Luther King Jr. did his job successfully in the 1960s, the next generation of civil rights leaders in the 1970s and beyond will build upon his words and work and extend them into new territory. The next generation will continue his work not by constantly repeating, "I have a dream," but by seizing the

new opportunities that arise precisely because Dr. King successfully articulated his dream.

Similarly, if Jesus does his job successfully, if Jesus effectively
proclaims and introduces and inducts people into the kingdom
of God, he bequeaths to his successors not the same situation he
inherited but rather a radically new situation—with new problems, new questions, new opportunities, and new requirements.
If we find Paul doing more than repeating the words and imagery
of Jesus, we shouldn't automatically conclude that Paul is preaching another message. Instead, we should consider that Paul may
be dealing faithfully with the new situation Jesus has created. In
this light, we can read Paul carefully and see if his message actually does deal with new problems and opportunities created by
Jesus' success.[2]

Jesus' secret message in word and deed makes clear that the
kingdom of God will be radically, scandalously inclusive. As
we've seen, Jesus enjoys table fellowship with prostitutes and
drunks, seeming to shift the locus of spirituality from the temple (which he says will be destroyed) to the table of fellowship
and reconciliation. He affirms and responds to the faith of
Gentiles—Romans and Syrophonecians and Samaritans. It takes
a while for his followers to realize where this will lead, but eventually they get it: they realize that in the kingdom of God, they
can no longer label people with old labels like male/female,
Jew/Gentile, slave/free, rich/poor, Barbarian/Scythian, and so on.
They must see people in a new light.[3] When they see people as
God's creations, beloved by the King and welcome in the kingdom, they must open their hearts, homes, tables, and fellowships
to everyone, without regard for old distinctions. That's radical
for everyone, but especially for Jesus' fellow Jews, whose unique
identity and devotion made them very suspicious of mixing with
non-Jews.

Right at the heart of Paul's letters, we find these very issues of inclusion played out time and again: How can Jews and Gentiles be brought together in one kingdom, one network of relationships? If Jewish followers of Jesus start associating, befriending, and—one must imagine gasps and shudders inserted here—eating with non-Jews, what do we do about practical matters, like the dietary restrictions that are so precious and important to Jewish people? If Gentiles who follow Jesus invite their Jewish colleagues over for dinner and serve them a ham casserole, do the Jewish guests leave in disgusted protest, politely refuse, or demonstrate their solidarity by violating their tradition and having seconds? Beyond religious scruples, how will rich and poor mix in these communities of the kingdom? Members of varied social classes and races? People with differing gifts, practices, and priorities? In letter after letter, Paul grapples with exactly these issues. A new and unprecedented social reality is being created—a new realm, a new network of relationships, a new kingdom.

So, beyond the thirteen direct references to the kingdom, we find in Paul's writings strong evidence that he is building on Jesus' foundation rather than laying a different foundation (1 Corinthians 3:11). But the question remains: if Paul doesn't use exactly the same language with similar frequency, how does he translate Jesus' message into his own, new situation?

CHAPTER 12

HIDING THE MESSAGE IN NEW PLACES

*The field is the world, and the good seed stands
for the sons of the kingdom.*

—Matthew 13:38

The great African theologian Lamin Sanneh points out that Christianity is unique among world religions for its amazing translatability. For example, it doesn't require that people of all cultures refer to God in the language of its founder or that they quote their founder in his original language. In fact, most of them don't even know what the language of the founder actually was![1] The religion, Sanneh says, takes on new languages and fresh imagery each time it enters a new culture. As we began to see in the preceding chapter, Paul—himself a boundary crosser—does much to translate Jesus' originally Jewish message so that non-Jews from around the Roman Empire can understand it as a live spiritual alternative.

For example, the empire of Rome was frequently depicted as the *body politic*, and Caesar was head of the body. Paul picks up the image and speaks of the body of Christ, with Christ as head.

Even Paul's oft-repeated language of Jesus being Lord resonates with kingdom language: the "pledge of allegiance" in the Roman Empire was (in Greek) *Caesar ho Kurios*—Caesar is Lord. To say Jesus is Lord is to declare one's allegiance to a different empire or kingdom, which is one reason that the early Christians were persecuted: not for their religious beliefs but for their lack of patriotism and national loyalty in refusing to say the expected "pledge of allegiance" to Caesar.

When you read Paul not just looking for overt kingdom references, but with this more general kingdom-consciousness in mind, his letters begin to sizzle and boil with resonance. Instead of the kingdom message of Jesus being downplayed, we realize it's there in powerful, unmistakable ways—but translated into different imagery. Take, for example, the poem (perhaps an early song lyric) Paul includes in the first section of his letter to the Colossians:[2]

> [Christ] is the image of the invisible God, the firstborn of all
>   creation;
> For in him all things in heaven and on earth were created,
> Things visible and invisible, whether thrones or dominions or
>   rulers or powers—
> All things have been created through him and for him.
> He himself is before all things, and in him all things hold
>   together.
> He is the head of the body, the church;
> He is the beginning, the firstborn from the dead,
> So that he might come to have first place in everything.
> For in him all the fullness of God was pleased to dwell,
> And through him God was pleased to reconcile to himself all things,
> Whether on earth or in heaven,
> By making peace through the blood of his cross. (Colossians
>   1:15–20 NRSV)

It doesn't take long to see how this poem throbs with the radical language of the kingdom of God and pulsates with the same kind of audacious, subversive confidence as the utterances of Jesus did.

Take the first line, about Jesus being the image of God. Many readers will recall how, after the fall of the Saddam Hussein regime in Iraq, news footage showed statues and paintings of the former dictator everywhere. The dictator had to maintain the constant illusion that "Uncle Saddam is watching you," and his regime did this by making Saddam's *image* ubiquitous—on buildings, in statues, on coins. In Jesus' day, the image of Caesar was similarly the omnipresent reminder of the Roman Empire (remember the question about whose image was on a coin?). But Paul suggests—as subtly as a parable, but unmistakably to be sure—that another kingdom is now at work on our planet. Its King is God, and God's image—the sign of God's present authority—is Jesus here among us.

How does a king or emperor ascend to the throne? By being the firstborn—and Paul twice proclaims Jesus as the firstborn: firstborn and heir of the original creation and firstborn and heir of the new creation, having died and been raised from death. A king's authority is absolute in his kingdom, and the word "all" echoes absolutely through the poem, asserting Jesus' unparalleled and unlimited authority. In fact, Paul says, in and through and for Christ, all systems of government were created—thrones, dominions, rulers, and powers—suggesting that Caesar and his kingdom actually exist in Jesus' territory rather than the reverse!

Caesar may claim to be the supreme and ultimate ruler, but Paul celebrates Jesus as being "before all things" and having "first place in everything." The Roman emperors claimed to be gods, but that's nothing, Paul implies, in comparison to this: all the fullness of one true and living God dwells in Jesus.

In the Roman Empire and, in a sense, in Caesar himself, diverse nations are brought together; his rule reconciles former enemies in the *Pax Romana*. But for Paul, it's not in Caesar but in Christ that all things are truly reconciled. And how is the *Pax Romana* enforced? By the threat of swift, horrible, lethal torture on a cross if anyone questions Roman supremacy—a threat graphically dramatized on many a roadside entering major cities throughout the empire. In other words, the Roman peace might be precious, but its cost is high—a lot of brutality, fear, violence, and blood are required to keep the peace. (St. Augustine, aware of this high and bloody cost, said the only difference between an emperor and a pirate is the number of his ships and weapons.)

And here, perhaps, is the most astounding contrast of all: the peace of God's kingdom comes not through the violent torture and merciless extermination of the king's enemies, but rather through the suffering and death of the king himself. The *pax Christi* is not the peace of conquest but rather the peace of true reconciliation. The king achieves peace not by shedding the blood of rebels but by—I hope the scandal and wonder of this is not lost because the words may be familiar—*shedding his own blood.*

And what is the goal of this suffering sacrifice, this self-giving to the point of blood to achieve the *pax Christi?* It is a new and lasting reconciliation between humanity and God, and among all the at-odds individuals and groups that comprise humanity. In another letter, Paul said it like this: "Old distinctions like Jew and Gentile, slave and free, male and female no longer exist, for you are all one in Christ" (see Galatians 3:28). Today, he might speak of reconciliation of the war veteran with the pacifist protester. The tattooed and pierced granddaughter with her prim and proper grandmother. The Orthodox with the Catholics, and Pentecostals with Baptists. Christians with Jews and Muslims and Hindus. Tutsi with Hutu and both with Twa.

Right-wing Republicans with left-wing Democrats. Believers with doubters.

What is this set of reconciled relationships other than the kingdom of God? Paul strikes the same theme in Ephesians 1:9–10: "[God] made known to us the mystery of his will according to his good pleasure, which he purposed in Christ, to be put into effect when the times will have reached their fulfillment— to bring unity to all things in heaven and on earth together under one head, even Christ." That unity—that bringing together under one head—is yet another translation of the kingdom of God.

Perhaps you noticed Paul's term for his message in the previous quote: *mystery*. In the writings attributed to him, Paul uses *mystery* as shorthand for his message fifteen times, including this instance in Colossians 1:27: "God chose to make known how great among the Gentiles are the riches of the glory of this *mystery*, which is Christ in you, the hope of glory" (ESV; emphasis added). Like Jesus, then, Paul has a secret message—a message that is both concealed and revealed. It is a message of reconciliation and unification, just as a kingdom brings people together under one king. It is, I propose, the same message—translated and extended into a new situation.

If that is the case, then we should be able to "untranslate" Paul's mystery (borrowing a bit from the preceding verses) and integrate it with Jesus' message of the kingdom like this:

> God has chosen to make known this great message, which had for long ages been a complete secret. It is an unprecedented, radically inclusive message. It is not just for the Jewish people but for people of all cultures. The secret is unspeakably rich and glorious, and here it is—the secret message, the mystery of the kingdom of God: that Christ the King indwells you, which

means that his kingdom is within and among you here and now. This secret message—Christ the King in and among us here and now—invites us into a reconciled and reconciling movement and expanding network of relationships. This is the glorious hope for which we have all been waiting for so long.

In spite of these synergies between Paul's mystery and Jesus' secret message, we must admit that Paul doesn't speak in parables as Jesus did.[3] But consider this: perhaps Paul doesn't need to use parables to illustrate and "hide" his message. Perhaps Paul himself is in fact a walking, talking parable traveling among other walking, talking communities of parables. Perhaps Paul's own story of transformation—from a hateful religious bigot to a bridge-building messenger of love and reconciliation—embodies and exemplifies the transforming and reconciling power of the good news of the kingdom. And perhaps the people he is gathering and networking are themselves—individually and as communities—a medium that contains the secret message of Jesus. Could it be that the message is hidden *in* them, in their common life, just as it was hidden in the parables of Jesus? Paul says as much in his second letter to the Corinthian church (3:2–3), when he tells them that they are a letter, an incarnated message, written not with ink but rather with the Spirit of the living God, not chiseled on stone tablets but embodied in living human hearts.

Let's think back to Paul's letter to the Colossians once more. Tucked away at the end of the letter hides this seemingly insignificant detail: someone named Onesimus accompanies the man who carries this letter. Onesimus is identified simply and warmly as "our faithful and dear brother" and "one of you" (4:9).

But here's the secret. That simple name telescopes into another whole story—a story that takes shape in another of Paul's letters, a short note to Philemon. There we learn that Onesimus was the slave of Philemon and that he ran away and ended up in jail with Paul. There, Paul introduced him to the good news of the kingdom of God. When Onesimus gained his freedom, Paul sent him back to his master with this plea: that Philemon would, "on the basis of love" rather than compulsion, do what he "ought to do," namely, welcome him "no longer as a slave, but better than a slave, as a dear brother . . . both as a man and as a brother in the Lord" (vv. 8–9, 16).

Yes, Jesus hid his message in parables: "The kingdom of God is like a man who planted a seed . . . It's like a man who had two sons . . . It's like a woman who put some yeast in some dough." But his message took root (like that seed), precipitated reconciliation (like that father and his younger son), and began infiltrating and transforming humanity (like yeast). And as a result, if you asked Paul, "What is the kingdom of God like?" he didn't need to repeat Jesus' parables. Instead, I have a hunch about what he would have said.

"Let me tell you a story about my dear friend Onesimus . . ." Or better yet, "Come with me to Colossae, and I'll introduce you to a community that includes two friends of mine, Onesimus and Philemon. I want you to get to know them and hear their story. Then you'll know what the kingdom of God is like."

Is this beginning to make sense? Can you see how the secret message of Jesus is meant not just to be heard or read but to be seen in human lives, in radically inclusive reconciling communities, written not on pages in a book but in the lives and hearts of friends? Can you see how the kingdom, originally hidden in parables, began to be hidden in new places—in the stories of real people and real communities across the Roman Empire and, eventually, around the world? Can you imagine yourself and your community of faith as a living parable where the secret message of Jesus could be hidden today?

I need to tell you that part of this chapter has been written through tears. I'm not exactly sure why I have felt so moved as I've written. I think it's a glimpse of the beauty of the secret message of Jesus.

CHAPTER 13

GETTING IT, GETTING IN

*Fear not, little flock, for it is your Father's good
pleasure to give you the kingdom.*
—LUKE 12:32 ESV

Imagine you live in Jesus' day. You've heard him speak. You've
seen him perform signs and wonders. You've maybe even had
a private conversation or two with him. What happens if you
start believing he's right and you want to sign on? How do you
get on the side of Jesus and his secret kingdom?

Or imagine you live today. (OK, that doesn't take any imagination.) You're reading this book, and you start getting a
glimpse of Jesus' message and its beauty. You realize that, yes,
you would like to live in a good and right interactive relationship with God as King and with all other people as your fellow
citizens. Jesus and his grand vision of the kingdom of God have
captured your heart and won your confidence. You would like
to be part of God's dream for our world coming true. The message is getting into you, and now you want to get into it. What
do you do?

How would a person make a move from where he or she is to where he or she wants to be, from the old confining kingdom of egotism, racism, consumerism, hedonism, and its other associated *-isms* to the expansive kingdom of God (in which, we might say, all those *-isms* are to become *-was-ms*)? When you look at Jesus' full range of teachings, it becomes clear that immigration into the kingdom—whether back then or now—would involve several interrelated moves.

The first move is to hear from the heart and to think deeply about what you hear. "All who have ears to hear," Jesus said, "let them hear." Hearing in this deep way means more than listening: it means thinking, and more than thinking. It means rethinking everything in light of the secret message. As we've seen, this profound rethinking is what the word *repent* means. It means that you begin looking at every facet of your life again in this new light—from the way you think about God to the way you treat your spouse, from your political affiliations to your spending habits, from what makes you angry to what makes you happy. It doesn't mean everything changes all at once, but it means you open up the possibility that everything may change over time. It involves a deep sense that you may be wrong, wrong about so much, along with the sincere desire to realign around what is good and true.

This repentance plays out humorously in this semifictional story.

It happened years ago, when I coached soccer for my kids. We were the mighty Yellow Jackets, an eight-and-under girls' team, and in our first few seasons we would lose by double-digit scores that seemed more like football scores: 21–3, 17–0, 28–4.

The girls liked each other so much, and they had so much fun just being together, they hardly noticed the score. Even after a trouncing, they'd run up to me, jumping and smiling and giggling. "Did we win? Did we win?" they would ask. "Well," I'd say, "we came in second."

During one game, Alexi, a good-natured and slightly chubby girl, was playing fullback. In an unusual moment of inspired intensity, she stole the ball and dribbled—or perhaps *chased* is a better word—the ball up to midfield. Soon she was swarmed by three skinny players from the other team, and they instantly formed a knot of eight kicking feet, eight flaring elbows, and four swaying ponytails. In the middle of the scramble, Alexi spun around a couple of times, trying to keep the ball in her control. When she broke free, a little dizzy, surprised to have the ball still in her control, she saw something she had never seen before: a wide open field between her and the goal.

I saw her glance up at the goal and then down at her feet, and I detected a look on her face I had never seen. It was as if, for the first time in this sport, she knew exactly what to do, and all her resources were unified in a glorious moment of clarity, hope, and commitment. She—a fullback—was going to score!

So she started dribbling. She had never dribbled so well. She drove forward, head down, fists clenched, deep in concentration. Kick, kick, step, kick, step, step, kick. There was only one problem in the entire universe at that moment, a problem of which she was blissfully unaware: *she was driving to the wrong goal.*

I started yelling, "Turn around! Turn around, Alexi! It's the wrong goal!" She plunged forward. Then the parents started shouting too. "Wrong way, Alexi! Wrong goal! Turn around!" She couldn't hear us; she was in another dimension of time and space. Her fellow defenders didn't want to steal the ball from their friend and teammate, so they backed away, confused. Kick, step,

step, kick, pause. She neared the goal and looked up once more, oblivious to our shouting, grim in her determination, pursing her lips. She was a fullback, a defender, and she had never been in scoring position before. Her latent inner athlete had come alive, and the thrill filled her with ecstasy. As her right foot cocked back in her backswing—the backswing of the most important kick of her entire eight-year life—somewhere in the inner regions of her brain a tiny alarm went off. *Why was her best friend and teammate Robin in the goal box? Why did Robin look so afraid?*

"No, Alexi! No!" Robin shouted. But it was too late. My husky little fullback was already in motion. The reflexes of her newly awakened inner athlete had clicked into motion and could not be stopped.

As her right foot came forward and connected with the ball, you could see the agony of an awful recognition spread across her face. First her expression and then her crumbling body folded into a living parable of repentance as she collapsed to the dirt. Her heart sank and the ball rose, sailing, sailing in a beautiful arc toward the net. Robin dove to her left, and at the last instant, the knuckles of her left fist grazed the ball so that it veered slightly to the right and down until it grazed the goalpost and dropped to the ground, rolling to a stop in a tuft of perfect green grass—just out of bounds. Robin had averted disaster for Alexi and for the Yellow Jackets. Her teammates, including Alexi, ran to her and tackled her in a joyful, shouting, screaming mass of relieved girlhood. Alexi's mistake was swallowed up in Robin's amazing save.

We lost 9–0 that day, but at least we were spared the indignity of scoring more points on our own goal than on theirs. At our awards banquet at the end of the season, Robin received the most valuable player trophy. Alexi presented it to her, beaming with pride because, in a way, the memory of her mistake was no longer her moment of shame: it was *their* moment of pride.

The story is fictional, although I did actually coach soccer, and we did indeed experience a few self-inflicted goals. But in real life, one of the most transforming things that can happen to any of us is to have a moment like Alexi's, where we realize that in spite of all our sincerity and drive, we're closing in on the wrong goal. And even better, to find out that our worst failure has been swallowed up in someone else's save. That's repentance.

I first reached this moment of repentance in my teenage years, but I have learned that really, once one begins repenting, it becomes a way of life. Once you've shot on your own goal, you're always aware that you might do it again, so you stay open to the possibility that no matter how sure of yourself you are, you may still be wrong. And once you've seen that someone else's save can overcome your wrong, you're well into the second move.

That second move—the move of faith, of believing, of trust-ing—flows so naturally within and from the first that it's hard to tell where one stops and the other starts. Once you have the capacity for self-doubt, you find yourself more able to trust God. Once you trust that God can "make a save," it's a lot easier to admit your own misdirection.

Now *believing* in this sense is not primarily *believing that*. It is more a matter of *believing in*, which presupposes the most impor-tant things *that* one might believe anyway. It's not simply believ-ing this or that *about* God; it's believing *in* God, or perhaps simply *believing* God with the kind of interpersonal confidence one has when saying, "I believe in my spouse." Equally, it's not simply believing this or that *about* the good news of the king-

dom; it's believing in or having confidence in the good news of
the kingdom.

How much must you believe? Is your believing disqualified
if you have X number of doubts? These questions haunt all of us
who are blessed and/or cursed with a highly reflective nature.
People like us are quite capable of doubting our own existence at
times, not to mention God's![1]

Jesus constantly dealt with this concern. It only takes a tiny
bit of faith, he said—faith the size of a mustard seed (which is
really small!). But how does one measure faith? Jesus answered
this as well: if you say you believe in his message, but you don't
seek to practice it, your faith is a matter of words only; it's not
substantial, not real. Faith that counts, then, is not the absence
of doubt; it's the presence of action. It puts you into motion,
propels you to action. As Jesus' early disciple Paul put it, "The
only thing that counts is faith expressing itself through love"
(Galatians 5:6). In this light, the phrase *leap of faith* isn't a leap
into faith; it's the leap that you take because you're already in
faith and want to put your faith into loving action. The little
boy who leaps from the stairway into his daddy's arms wouldn't
leap unless he were, in a certain sense, already securely and con-
fidently there in those arms in his imagination. Once the deed
is safely done in his imagination, the actual leap is pure, exhila-
rating joy.

The third move, which itself grows out of rethinking and
faith, is out of your control, really, yet it requires something of
you. If you repent and believe, you must stay open to receive.
Receptivity is hard to define. It's not exactly active, and neither
is it passive. I suppose it's a lot like a woman who wants to get
pregnant. There's only so much she can do, and it all boils down
to receptivity.

This receptivity, by the way, is the best reason Christians

have for revering Mary, Jesus' mother. As you'll recall from the Christmas story, Mary was confronted with the hard-to-believe news that she would become pregnant. This required a kind of repentance (rethinking what was possible and impossible for a virgin like herself). It required faith. And then it required receptivity, an openness to receive. She expressed this receptivity in the words "let it be"—words that John Lennon may have made more famous than Mary: "Let it be to me according to your word" (Luke 1:38 ESV).

What is it that you receive? It's not just one thing, really. It's more like everything: forgiveness, acceptance, love, hope, empowerment, strength, encouragement, perseverance, everything you need to live in the kingdom of God. It's more than these things too: what we really need to receive, according to Jesus, is God's Spirit. As a parent gladly showers a beloved child with good gifts, God somehow wants to give the best possible gift to us—God's own self. So we open our hearts to receive everything we need for life in the kingdom of God, including God's own Spirit. This "everything . . . including God's Spirit" is what Jesus was talking about when he said, "Fear not, little flock, for it is your Father's good pleasure to give you the kingdom" (Luke 12:32 ESV). Without this third move—this cultivation of receptivity—we always run the risk of thinking the kingdom is something we *achieve* by earning, rather than a gift we *receive* by grace alone.

The fourth move flows naturally from the first three. It is a move of going public with your repentance, faith, and receptivity. In Jesus' day, the way you went public was through baptism. Baptism was a ceremonial washing—symbolically expressing your belief that you had previously been dirty and now you wanted to be cleansed. It symbolized the moves of repentance ("I'm washing away my old life—even burying it"), faith ("I trust Christ enough to follow him in his kingdom"), and receptivity ("I receive God's own Spirit and all God wants to give me").

Religious people today may differ on how much water should be used (A few drops? A pitcher full? A river or pond into which you are plunged?), but my sense is that the amount of water is less important than the amount of commitment and sincerity with which you choose to go public and identify with Jesus, with the kingdom of God, and with others who are seeking the kingdom with you.

These four moves are really preparations for the fifth and most comprehensive move, a move in which you will be engaged for the rest of your life: to learn to follow Jesus every day over the whole course of your life. In other words, you don't simply move into a new *status* like becoming a member of a club. No, more—you move into a new *practice*, like a doctor entering the practice of medicine, a lawyer entering the practice of law, a student entering the practice of martial arts, or an artist entering the practice of sculpture. You are now launching out on a new way of life, a new vocation, centered on the practice of Jesus' message. Jesus put it like this: as a new disciple, you learn to *practice everything he has taught* (Matthew 28:18–20).

As with medicine, law, art, music, martial arts, or any other practice, you develop your skill through applying yourself to *practices* (or disciplines). As we'll see in an upcoming chapter, these practices will include things like giving to the poor, praying, and fasting. They work like exercise: as you practice the practices, your "muscles" develop—your capacities increase—so that you become a person capable of doing new things you couldn't do before, of living a new way of life you couldn't have lived before.

Let's create a parable (actually, it's more of an allegory) at this point to integrate these five moves into one movement. Entering the kingdom of God, we could say, is like immigrating to a new country . . .

A friend returns from vacation and tells you about this new land she has seen, and it sounds absolutely wonderful. You've always been more or less satisfied with your fatherland: it is the only reality you have ever imagined. But her stories make you notice things you never noticed before. Compared to the new land your friend has described, your fatherland suffers from stifling air pollution; the scenery is blah; the culture is boring, crude, and uncreative; and the economy is stagnant. The more you replay the scenes and stories described by your friend—stories of exciting people, vibrant culture, beautiful scenery, and a robust economy—the more you feel restless. One evening, your dinner is interrupted by six successive calls from telemarketers selling gas masks so you can breathe more easily on high-pollution days, and something in you snaps. *That's it! I've had it! I'm leaving!* you think. *I'm going to start a new life in this new land my friend has told me about.*

So you gradually begin to imagine life in the new kingdom. Gradually, you can see yourself there—and life is better. Still, you vacillate for a while. Do you have enough faith to pack your suitcase and head to the border? Do you really trust your friend enough to make a move like this? You share with her your dreams—and your doubts—and she says, "If you go, I'll go with you. Ever since I visited, I can't stop thinking about going back for good." And that tips the balance. You sell your house and all your possessions, and the two of you set off.

With some apprehension, you approach the border. You present your papers and declare yourself an immigrant. They ask you one simple question: "Do you wish to leave your past behind and start a new life in our kingdom?" When you say yes, they issue you a passport—no questions asked—and then they recommend that you take a bath. They explain that immigrants usually find it wise to wash off the soot and smell of their old country so they can have a clean start in this new homeland. You comply, and you're glad you did. You step outside and take a deep breath, and your lungs feel as if you're inhaling pure health, joy, and peace. It's as if the spirit of the new kingdom is entering you. You feel alive as never before.

You find a new home, meet your new neighbors, and settle into a whole new life. You quickly realize you have a lot to learn. The people speak a new dialect here. It's not the old familiar accent of pride, judgment, bragging, misleading, insulting, or lying; rather, it's an accent of gratitude, encouragement, truth telling, admitting faults, celebrating joys. You also notice that people here live at a different pace than you're used to—they're not lazy, and they're not workaholics either. They live with a certain rhythm, weaving rest and work and worship and play and fellowship and sacrifice and feasting and fasting. As you settle into your new life, you almost feel that you have been born into a new autobiography and a new world.

Rethinking, believing, receiving, going public, and practicing a new way of life—these seem to be the basic elements of what it means to get in on the secret and let it get into you.

PART 3

IMAGINATION:

EXPLORING HOW JESUS' SECRET MESSAGE
COULD CHANGE EVERYTHING

CHAPTER 14

KINGDOM MANIFESTO

*Not every one who says to me, "Lord, Lord," will enter
the kingdom of heaven, but only he who does the will of
my Father who is in heaven.*

—MATTHEW 7:21

If you say, "I'm in. I want to enter the kingdom of God and
learn its ways," what then? Where do you go to learn?[1] In
Jesus' day, you would have gone out to the countryside or the
temple courts or wherever Jesus was teaching. Where do you go
today to find Jesus' teaching on the kingdom?

The most concentrated example of the teaching of Jesus is
found in Matthew 5–7, a passage often called the Sermon on the
Mount, but which we'll call Jesus' kingdom manifesto. In some
ways, it is untypical of Jesus' communication style because it is
an extended monologue rather than the more typical dialogue.
Also, it contains no parables, although it is full of other brilliant
literary and rhetorical devices. It is therefore an unusual—perhaps *unique* is a better word—example of Jesus' teaching. If we
want to understand certain essential facets of Jesus' secret message, there's no better place to go than here.

I should acknowledge that many people assume the sermon intends to answer one question—namely, "How does an individual go to heaven after death?" This was my assumption as well for many years, but as I have reflected on the life and message of Jesus, I have become convinced that Jesus is exploring a very different set of questions—namely, "What kind of life does God want people to live? What does life in the kingdom of God look like? What is a truly good (or righteous) life? How does this message differ from conventional messages?" Rather than directing our attention to life after death in heaven, away from this life and beyond history, these questions return our focus to the here and now—and in so doing, they provide an essential window into Jesus' secret message.

The story begins with Jesus sitting on a hillside. You'll remember that in those days, the teacher would sit and the students would stand, which would no doubt decrease the chances of students falling asleep. But given the riveting, revolutionary nature of Jesus' message, that wasn't a great danger. The sitting posture also suggested that the teacher is at rest (not needing to entertain, as is so often the case with today's teachers), and it's the students who must be on tiptoe, so to speak, eager to learn the treasures held in the teacher's mind and heart. So Jesus takes a seat—perhaps on a rock jutting out from the Middle Eastern landscape—and he gathers his disciples around him as his primary hearers, with the crowds in a sense eavesdropping.

Jesus begins with what people often call the "Beatitudes"—eight statements that tell what kinds of people, in Jesus' perspective, are well off, have "the good life," are fortunate and blessed. From the first statement, they turn normal expectations upside down. Instead of what we might expect—"Blessed are the rich, blessed are the happy, blessed are the bold, blessed are the satisfied, blessed are the winners, blessed are the clever, blessed are the victors, and blessed are the safe and well-respected"—Jesus says the opposite:

> Blessed are the poor in spirit, for theirs is the kingdom of heaven.
> Blessed are those who mourn, for they will be comforted.
> Blessed are the meek, for they will inherit the earth.
> Blessed are those who hunger and thirst for righteousness, for
> they will be filled.
> Blessed are the merciful, for they will receive mercy.
> Blessed are the pure in heart, for they will see God.
> Blessed are the peacemakers, for they will be called children of God.
> Blessed are those who are persecuted for righteousness' sake, for
> theirs is the kingdom of heaven.
> Blessed are you when people revile you and persecute you and
> utter all kinds of evil against you falsely on my account.
> Rejoice and be glad, for your reward is great in heaven, for
> in the same way they persecuted the prophets who were
> before you. (Matthew 5:3–12 NRSV)

This introduction does several things. First, it grabs the hearers' attention with a kind of mystique, intrigue, and perhaps shock. We can imagine Jesus' hearers thinking, *Blessed are the poor? Those who mourn? What?* Second, it moves from the general "blessed are they" to the personal "blessed are you," bringing hearers deeper and more personally into Jesus' circle. Third, it sets up a tension— a tension that seems inherent throughout Jesus' teachings— between peace (blessed are the meek, the peacemakers, the pure in heart) and conflict (with persecution, insult, false accusation). In other words, Jesus here sets the stage for talking about his radical, surprising, unexpected, and counterintuitive kingdom—a kingdom that seems to turn normal perception and standard common sense upside down.

Jesus builds on this disruption: his followers are not simply normal people with a certain religious preference. No, they are radical participants in a high-commitment endeavor—compared to salt, which flavors and preserves meat, and to light, which penetrates and eradicates darkness:

> You are the salt of the earth; but if salt has lost its taste, how can its saltiness be restored? It is no longer good for anything, but is thrown out and trampled under foot.
>
> You are the light of the world. A city built on a hill cannot be hid. No one after lighting a lamp puts it under the bushel basket, but on the lampstand, and it gives light to all in the house. In the same way, let your light shine before others, so that they may see your good works and give glory to your Father in heaven. (vv. 13–16 NRSV)

To this point, Jesus hasn't used the word *kingdom*, but now he does—three times, after throwing down a gauntlet of sorts. The logic of this paragraph is intriguing. We generally make our points and then qualify them, but Jesus first makes the qualifications and then makes his bold point at the end:

> Do not think that I have come to abolish the law or the prophets; I have come not to abolish but to fulfill. For truly I tell you, until heaven and earth pass away, not one letter, not one stroke of a letter, will pass from the law until all is accomplished. Therefore, whoever breaks one of the least of these commandments, and teaches others to do the same, will be called least in the kingdom of heaven; but whoever does them and teaches them will be called great in the kingdom of heaven. For I tell you, unless your righteousness exceeds that of the scribes and Pharisees, you will never enter the kingdom of heaven. (vv. 17–20 NRSV)

This last statement—if there is anything like a thesis statement to this sermon—would probably earn that title. The scribes (or religious scholars) and the Pharisees are seen as—and see themselves as—the guardians and paragons of personal piety, goodness, morality, uprightness, decency, justice, and fairness (all of which seem to be wrapped up in the complex and pregnant word *righteousness*). It would be scandalous, perhaps even ridiculous to suggest that the Scribes and Pharisees are not entering the kingdom and that those who wish to enter the kingdom must do better they.

These words would be profoundly disruptive—and insulting—to these religious leaders and to others who were similarly snug and smug in their insider status. No wonder Jesus begins by affirming his fidelity to the Jewish Sacred Writings. No wonder he pledges that he has not come to abolish the Sacred Writings—not to break them, annul them, or water them down (although he will be accused of these very things)—but to fulfill them.

But what does it mean to fulfill? Jesus makes it clear with a series of examples that follow. Each example begins, "You have heard that it was said," which introduces what the Law and Prophets and Jewish tradition have taught. Then Jesus says, "But I say to you," and what follows is an invitation not to lower standards but to raise them, deepen them, fulfill them—to take them above the level of the religious scholars and Pharisees, from the level of external conformity to internal change of mind and heart:

> You have heard that it was said to those of ancient times, "You shall not murder"; and "whoever murders shall be liable to judgment." But I say to you that if you are angry with a brother or sister, you will be liable to judgment; and if you insult a brother or sister, you will be liable to the council; and if you say, "You fool," you will be liable to the hell of fire. (vv. 21–22 NRSV)

Ancient wisdom forbade murder, but Jesus' message, the message of the kingdom of God, calls people deeper and higher: to transcend the hidden emotion of anger that motivates murder and to stop insulting people. After all, insult is a kind of character assassination, a kind of socially acceptable violence with words. The kingdom of God calls us beyond simply "doing no physical harm" (as big an improvement as that is over doing physical harm!); it calls us to do no harm with words. And even more radical—it calls us to actively seek reconciliation, giving interpersonal reconciliation an even higher priority than religious devotion as the next few sentences make clear:

> So when you are offering your gift at the altar, if you remember that your brother or sister has something against you, leave your gift there before the altar and go; first be reconciled to your brother or sister, and then come and offer your gift. Come to terms quickly with your accuser while you are on the way to court with him, or your accuser may hand you over to the judge, and the judge to the guard, and you will be thrown into prison. Truly I tell you, you will never get out until you have paid the last penny. (vv. 23–26 NRSV)

Even though Jesus uses dangerous, provocative language—"You have heard that it was said . . . but I say to you"—this is no abolishment of the Sacred Writings. No, Jesus is calling people to a higher way of life that both fulfills the intent of the Law and exceeds the rigor of the religious scholars and Pharisees, who focus on a merely external conformity and technical perfection. As the manifesto continues, Jesus applies the same "You have heard . . . but I say" pattern to deeply important issues for individuals and societies—sexuality, marriage, oaths, and revenge.

In each case, conventional religious morality ("the righteousness of the scribes and Pharisees") is about *not doing external wrong*: not murdering, not committing adultery, not committing divorce, not breaking sacred oaths, not getting revenge on the wrong people. But the kingdom manifesto calls us beyond and beneath this kind of morality; we must deal with greed and lust, arrogance and prejudice in the heart. And more, instead of merely not doing wrong, with a changed heart we will be motivated to do what is right. Jesus' words on adultery fit into this pattern. Yes, he says, you can avoid technically committing adultery, but your heart can be full of lust. Just as there would be no murder without anger, there would be no adultery without lust. So, Jesus says, if you want to live in the kingdom of God, you don't seek to stir up lust and then prevent adultery, but rather you seek to deal with the root, the source. The kingdom of God calls you to desire and seek a genuinely pure heart.

Or, if you are a man (only men could sue for divorce in those days), you can get a "perfectly" legal divorce so everything is externally okay, just like someone who never commits murder or adultery. That's completely satisfactory for "the righteousness of the scribes and Pharisees." But the kingdom of God goes further and says, "No. You can be legal, but your legal divorce causes trouble for your ex-wife, so that doesn't fly in the kingdom of God. That 'righteousness' isn't righteous enough."

But Jesus' next move is surprising. It's clear that he's still thinking about sexual fidelity, because he'll return to that subject immediately, but first he inserts this odd exhortation:

> If your right eye causes you to sin, tear it out and throw it away; it is better for you to lose one of your members than for your whole body to be thrown into hell. And if your right hand causes you to sin, cut it off and throw it away; it is better

for you to lose one of your members than for your whole body
to go into hell. (vv. 29–30 NRSV)

Jesus may simply be using the grotesque imagery of physical
self-mutilation to convey the horror of self-inflicted spiritual
mutilation by lust. But he may be doing something even more
subversive. He has just suggested that the way of the kingdom
goes deeper than mere outward conformity; it deals with internal motivations, not just external behaviors. But now he seems to
reverse himself, conjuring the most grossly superficial and external image possible: of avoiding doing wrong by amputating
body parts! Philosopher Dallas Willard, I think, rightly captures
Jesus' actual strategy:

> If not doing anything wrong is the goal, that could be
> achieved by dismembering yourself and making actions
> impossible. What you cannot do you certainly will not do.
> Remove your eye, your hand, etc., therefore, and you will roll
> into heaven a mutilated stump. The price of dismemberment
> would be small compared to the reward of heaven. That is the
> logical conclusion for one who held the beliefs of the scribes
> and the Pharisees. . . . He reduces their principle—that righ-
> teousness lies in not doing anything wrong—to the absurd, in
> the hope that they will forsake their principle and see and
> enter the righteousness that is "beyond the righteousness of
> the scribes and Pharisees"—beyond, where compassion or love
> and not sacrifice is the fundamental thing.[2]

Jesus continues the pattern of going beyond conventional
morality in his analysis of swearing oaths. People on the level of
the scribes and Pharisees may argue about which kinds of vows
are legitimate: it's easy to imagine a "liberal" wing and a "conserva-

tive" wing engaged in hot debate on the subject. But the kingdom of God raises the level of discourse to a higher plane entirely: What are the unintended negative consequences of vows? Why make vows at all? Jesus suggests that making vows can trick us into thinking we have more power than we actually have. So the king-dom of God raises the standard and requires more modest, simple speech. The same pattern holds true for revenge, an especially hot topic for people offended by Roman occupation:

> You have heard that it was said, "An eye for an eye and a tooth for a tooth." But I say to you, Do not [violently] resist an evil-doer. But if anyone strikes you on the right cheek, turn the other also; and if anyone wants to sue you and take your coat, give your cloak as well; and if anyone forces you to go one mile, go also the second mile. Give to everyone who begs from you, and do not refuse anyone who wants to borrow from you. (vv. 38–42 NRSV)

Conventional morality argues for appropriate revenge (an eye for an eye), but Jesus calls for something beyond revenge entirely: reconciliation. These are the words that so inspired Gandhi, Martin Luther King Jr., Desmond Tutu, Nelson Mandela, the people of post-genocide Rwanda, and so many others. These words introduced radical new ways of responding to injustice: nonviolent resistance, conflict transformation, and active peace-making. Think of it like this:

If someone strikes you on the right cheek, they have given you a backhand slap—the kind of thing a person in power (like a Roman soldier) does to a person he considers inferior (like a Jew). You could strike back, but that would reduce you to the same vio-lent level as your oppressor. Or you could simply skulk away in humiliation, but that would mean letting the oppressor win. The kingdom manifesto invites you to pursue a third alternative: courageously turn the other cheek. Think of it: now to strike you on the left cheek, your presumably right-handed oppressor must treat you not as an inferior person but as a peer by hitting you with his fist, not his backhand. You have shown yourself to be not violent or weak but rather courageous and dignified and strong. You have shown your oppressor for the violent person he is. You have thus transcended oppression without violence or revenge.

Similarly, if someone takes you to court—as rich landowners would often do to poor peasants who had gotten in debt—and they want your outer garment, Jesus says to strip down naked and give them your underwear as well! Your "generosity" leaves you defenseless and exposed—but in a sense, your exposure exposes the naked greed and cruelty of your oppressors. Again, you have transcended oppression without violence. (No doubt, this would have gotten a good laugh as people pictured it.)

Or if someone forces you to carry his pack a mile—which a Roman soldier could do to any Jew—by willingly taking the pack the second mile, you show yourself a generous human being, strong, self-controlled, dignified, not dominated. The first mile may be forced, but the second mile, you walk free—transcending your oppression. The way to transcend a corrupt system is through generosity—giving, not holding back.

I don't believe these are simple rules. After all, if people being sued predictably stripped naked in court, magistrates would simply pass an antinakedness law, and the response would lose its effect. Rather, they are examples of the active, creative, transforming ways of the kingdom of God—overcoming violence not with violence but with creativity and generosity.[3]

Again, the familiar pattern of Jesus' kingdom manifesto crescendos to its climax in the next few sentences:

You have heard that it was said, "You shall love your neighbor and hate your enemy." But I say to you, Love your enemies and pray for those who persecute you, so that you may be children of your Father in heaven; for he makes his sun rise on the evil and on the good, and sends rain on the righteous and on the unrighteous. For if you love those who love you, what reward do you have? Do not even the tax collectors do the same? And if you greet only your brothers and sisters, what more are you doing than others? Do not even the Gentiles do the same? Be perfect, therefore, as your heavenly Father is perfect. (vv. 43–48 NRSV)

This is one of the most powerful—yet misunderstood— passages in biblical literature, misunderstood largely because people neglect Jesus' larger-scale strategy in this whole sermon. They assume (just as the religious scholars and Pharisees may have, by the way) that "Be perfect" means "Achieve external technical perfection." In context, though, it's abundantly clear that Jesus means something poles apart from external technical perfection:

The kingdom of God calls you to a higher way of living. It's not just about loving friends and hating enemies. It's about loving your enemies. This is what the King does, so this is the way of the kingdom. God is good to all—including evil people. God's perfection is a compassionate perfection. That's the kind of love you need to have in God's kingdom—a compassionate perfection that transcends old divisions of us/them and neighbor/enemy, that loves those who do not yet love you. We will never reach universal reconciliation in the kingdom of God until we move beyond conventional religious morality and believe in and practice this radical, higher plan.

The parallel passage in Luke 6 substitutes the word "compassionate (of merciful)" for "perfect," strongly reinforcing this reading.

Now, recalling the political context of Roman occupation and the varied contemporary agendas for Jewish liberation, Jesus' understanding of the kingdom here is guaranteed to satisfy nobody. Those who believe in "redemptive violence"—that the kingdom will come through shedding the blood of enemies—will be disgusted. Those who believe that the best path is to compromise and adapt to the status quo will find Jesus' words unsettling and therefore unsatisfactory. And the scribes and Pharisees are probably still stinging from Jesus' earlier "thesis statement." Their blood pressure may never be the same after being marginalized by Jesus' direct rejection of their "righteousness" and by his implication that they are in fact not operating within the kingdom of God and need to enter it by following his different and better way.

If there is a point in this book where readers might be tempted to slam the cover shut and say, "This is ridiculous. This is unrealistic. This is a pipe dream. Nothing like this could ever happen," this would be that point. Perhaps they would be right in doing so. But what do they have to look forward to if they're right? Simply more of the same in human history, on the level of individuals, families, and nations—more of the cycle of offense and revenge, undertaken with more and more powerful weapons, with more and more at stake in each confrontation.

What would it mean if, at this moment, many readers actually began to believe that another world is possible, that Jesus may in fact have been right, that the secret message of the kingdom of God—though radical, though unprecedented in its vision, though requiring immense faith to believe it is possible—may in fact be the only authentically saving message we have?

CHAPTER 15

KINGDOM ETHICS

Therefore whoever relaxes one of the least of these commandments
and teaches others to do the same will be called least in the
kingdom of heaven, but whoever does them and teaches them
will be called great in the kingdom of heaven.
—Matthew 5:19 ESV

Not only does Jesus' kingdom manifesto transform social relationships, but it also transforms what we might call spiritual practices. As in previous sections of the manifesto, Jesus has a main point and again follows a repeated pattern to make it. This time it isn't "You have heard that it was said . . . But I say to you." This time it's "Whenever you . . . do not . . . but instead." The "whenever" introduces a spiritual practice. The "do not" introduces a warning about how the practice can be—and typically is—abused and rendered ineffective. The "but instead" describes a healthy and transformative approach to the spiritual practice.

A full exploration of spiritual practices lies beyond our scope here, but a brief analogy might be helpful. I can run a mile. I'm not in the greatest of physical shape, but I can do it. I can't run a marathon. It wouldn't matter how serious I am, how desperate I am, how sincere I am—no matter how hard I try, I will cramp up, go into cardiac arrest, collapse due to fatigue, or in some other way prove myself incapable of running 26.2 miles. But, as thousands of people have learned, what is presently impossible to me could become possible if I would begin to follow the practices of marathon runners—namely, running short distances and gradually increasing them over a period of weeks or months. Through research (including a lot of trial and error), people in the tradition of marathon running have learned various patterns of practice so that they can do what was previously impossible.[1]

Spiritual practices work in similar ways. Just as running practitioners have developed time-tested regimens or protocols that will guide the beginner into the ways of marathon runners, so have spiritual practitioners created what we could call *spiritual traditions* for spiritual transformation. One begins a lumpy couch potato and can end up a marathon runner; one begins an obnoxious or depressed egotist and ends up a loving, kind, and mature citizen of the kingdom of God. Without the benefit of the tradition, however, one could easily train unwisely, even counterproductively, and not reap the hoped-for rewards of practice. "Practice makes perfect" isn't quite accurate. Practice makes *habitual*, so unwise or misguided practice can make the practitioner miserably habituated in unrewarding routines. In contrast, wise practice rewards the practitioner by making possible what was previously impossible.

In his kingdom manifesto, Jesus identifies ways in which "the righteousness of the scribes and Pharisees" counterproductively habituates people in corrupted practices. He focuses on three practices, beginning with *giving to the poor*:

> Beware of practicing your piety before others in order to be seen by them; for then you have no reward from your Father in heaven.

So whenever you give alms, do not sound a trumpet before you, as the hypocrites do in the synagogues and in the streets, so that they may be praised by others. Truly I tell you, they have received their reward. But when you give alms, do not let your left hand know what your right hand is doing, so that your alms may be done in secret; and your Father who sees in secret will reward you. (Matthew 6:1–4 NRSV)

He follows the same pattern regarding *prayer*:

And whenever you pray, do not be like the hypocrites; for they love to stand and pray in the synagogues and at the street corners, so that they may be seen by others. Truly I tell you, they have received their reward. But whenever you pray, go into your room and shut the door and pray to your Father who is in secret; and your Father who sees in secret will reward you.

When you are praying, do not heap up empty phrases as the Gentiles do; for they think that they will be heard because of their many words. Do not be like them, for your Father knows what you need before you ask him. (vv. 5–8 NRSV)

Here Jesus inserts additional training on prayer. Then he returns to his pattern—this time regarding *fasting*: "Whenever you . . . do not . . . but do":

And whenever you fast, do not look dismal, like the hypocrites, for they disfigure their faces so as to show others that they are fasting. Truly I tell you, they have received their reward. But when you fast, put oil on your head and wash your face, so that your fasting may be seen not by others but by your Father who is in secret; and your Father who sees in secret will reward you. (vv. 16–18 NRSV)

This language of secrecy resonates with the entire message of Jesus. His kingdom is not about a show. It's not about high volume and hype, glitzy spectacle, or impressive appearances. No, the reverse: it is understated, secret, behind the scenes. Its rewards come not through public talk but through potent, private practice. Similarly, he says, our wealth should be behind the scenes; we should "store up treasures in heaven":

> Do not store up for yourselves treasures on earth, where moth and rust consume and where thieves break in and steal; but store up for yourselves treasures in heaven, where neither moth nor rust consumes and where thieves do not break in and steal. For where your treasure is, there your heart will be also.
>
> The eye is the lamp of the body. So, if your eye is healthy, your whole body will be full of light; but if your eye is unhealthy, your whole body will be full of darkness. If then the light in you is darkness, how great is the darkness!
>
> No one can serve two masters; for a slave will either hate the one and love the other, or be devoted to the one and despise the other. You cannot serve God and wealth. (vv. 19–24 NRSV)

Here again the kingdom of God clearly confronts the kingdoms of our world today. How often do our lives revolve around status-oriented accumulation and conspicuous consumption? In that context, Jesus' words about our *eyes being unhealthy* seem to have a special resonance in our world. We are daily massaged by a hyperactive consumerist vision to see and measure everything in life in terms of money—so that, as everyone knows, even *time is money*. With that kind of unhealthy, shady outlook, all of life falls into a kind of dismal shadow, just as Jesus said it would.

Perhaps it now becomes clear why giving to the poor begins Jesus' list of spiritual practices: if we are to experience spiritual transformation so that we can become the kinds of people whose "righteousness" transcends the mere avoidance of doing wrong, mere technical perfection and external conformity—then we must be liberated from enslavement to money. Perhaps the irony hits you, as it does me, that the people of Jesus' day are pre-occupied by the Roman occupation, but perhaps it is another empire—the empire of money and greed—that has even more power over them (and us) than Caesar ever could.

Jesus uses this very language of power and domination in this section of the manifesto. You can't serve two masters, he says. You can't be a citizen of the kingdom of God while you also bow the knee to an economic Caesar. Money, it turns out, is a cruel task-master; when you serve money, soon you will resent God for inter-fering with your humming, expanding economic kingdom. Similarly, if you serve God, you will soon resent wealth for its con-stant guerilla warfare, its subtle invasion of every sector of life, its relentless conquest of life's nonmaterial values. You have to choose.

It's fascinating to stop at this point in the sermon and catch our breath. What have been the key issues Jesus has addressed in his kingdom manifesto? To what themes has he returned? First, of course, is *money*—which is itself about values. From the seem-ingly absurd proposition that blessing is associated with poverty of spirit (or simple poverty in Luke's version) to this binary option between serving God and wealth, Jesus makes it clear that the kingdom of God presents us with a radically different value system than we see in the world around us. Second, as we might expect, is *sex*. From saying, "Blessed are the pure in heart," through his teaching about the power of lust in the heart, to his words about the unexpected negative consequences of even legal divorces, Jesus proposes a kingdom that is a matter of the heart, not the pelvis. And third, from his blessing of the meek and persecuted to his warnings about insult and anger, to his exposure of hypocritical external displays of piety, including his words about making oaths, Jesus is concerned about *power*—how we use violence, language, and even religion to dominate others and secure our own superior status.

The kingdom of God, then, is a revolutionary, counter-cultural movement—proclaiming a ceaseless rebellion against the tyrannical trinity of money, sex, and power. Its citizens resist the occupation of this invisible Caesar through three categories of spiritual practice. First, they practice a liberating *generosity toward the poor* to dethrone greed and topple the regime of money. Second, they practice a kind of *prayer* that is a defiant act of resistance against the prideful pursuit of power, pursuing forgiveness and reconciliation, not retaliation and revenge. Finally, they practice *fasting* to revolt against the dominating impulses of physical gratification—so that the sex drive and other physical appetites will not become our slave drivers. And all of these are practiced covertly, *in secret*, so they aren't corrupted into an external show "as the hypocrites do."

When we live for money, sex, and power, we will always experience anxiety, and Jesus turns to this subject next. He invites us to consider wildflowers and common birds—one imagines him pointing to some growing nearby or flying overhead as he speaks—reminding us that God cares for them and we are more valuable to God than they are. So why worry? I am tempted here to go on a long excursion about how this section of the manifesto invites us to conceive of the kingdom of God as a beautiful web of kinship that, in ways that St. Francis saw more clearly than we normally do, makes birds and flowers our sisters and brothers. We could explore the spirituality of ecology in this context and conceive of the kingdom as the ultimate ecosystem that integrates all of life—the parts that we would call scientific and physical and the parts that we would call spiritual and invisible.

But that would be an excursion from the main thrust of Jesus' line of thought here, which addresses the anxiety we feel when money, sex, and power hold our attention and affection rather than God and God's kingdom.

Anxiety about this stuff is a waste of time, Jesus says. And worse, it distracts us from what matters most. "Is not life more important than food," he asks, "and the body more important than clothes?" (v. 25). If you are confident that "your heavenly Father knows that you need" food, drink, clothing (v. 32), then you can focus on the most important thing of all. What is that? We shouldn't be surprised at Jesus' climactic answer—it's the kingdom of God: "But seek first [God's] kingdom and his right-eousness, and all these things [food, clothing, etc.] will be given to you as well" (v. 33). There's a way of living that surpasses that of the religious scholars and Pharisees, Jesus has promised. It's the life of seeking first God's kingdom—of making God's king-dom our first priority.

In the remainder of the manifesto, he will explore more of what that life entails, focusing on how we treat others, how we trust God, and how we go beyond superficial words to substan-tive action. It makes sense at this point for us to summarize the practical, ethical implications of the sermon as a whole:[2]

> Be poor in spirit, mourn, be meek, hunger and thirst for true
> righteousness, be merciful, be pure in heart, be a peace-
> maker, be willing to joyfully suffer persecution and insult for
> doing what is right.
> Be salt and light in the world—by doing good works.
> Do not hate or indulge in anger, but instead seek to reconcile.
> Do not lust or be sexually unfaithful in your heart.
> Do not presume to make vows, but have simple speech, where
> yes means yes and no, no.

Do not get revenge, but find creative and nonviolent ways to
    overcome evil done to you.
Love your enemies, as God does, and be generous to everyone,
    as God is.
Give to the poor, pray, and fast secretly.
Don't let greed cloud your outlook, but store up treasure in
    heaven through generosity.
Don't worry about your own daily needs, but instead trust your-
    self to God's care, and seek God's kingdom first and foremost.
Don't judge others, but instead first work on your own blindness.
Go to God with all your needs, knowing that God is a caring
    Father.
Do to others as you would have them do to you.
Don't be misled by religious talk; what counts is actually living
    by Jesus' teaching.

Jesus reinforces this last point—that he's looking for action,
not just agreement—in the final words of the manifesto:

Everyone then who hears these words of mine and acts on
them will be like a wise man who built his house on rock. The
rain fell, the floods came, and the winds blew and beat on that
house, but it did not fall, because it had been founded on rock.
And everyone who hears these words of mine and does not act
on them will be like a foolish man who built his house on sand.
The rain fell, and the floods came, and the winds blew and
beat against that house, and it fell—and great was its fall!
(Matthew 7:24–27 NRSV)

Once again, there may be a primarily political dimension to
this story. The Jewish people may reject the message they have
just heard, and if they do, if they instead follow a path of violent

revolution, their house will crash when the storm of Roman retaliation comes on them. But if they choose Jesus' path, whatever the Romans do, they will survive and stand strong. But beyond that immediate political point, the general meaning remains for all of us: what counts is fruit, action, putting his message into practice, building a way of life upon this message.

There is a certain foreboding in the final image of Jesus' kingdom manifesto: we see a house collapsing in a storm. The image contrasts so starkly with his words just a few minutes earlier— about living carefree like sparrows and wildflowers, secure in the care of God. It's a disturbing way to end a message. It doesn't leave us feeling good; it leaves us knowing that we have a choice.

That's why I don't think we can move on from this point without asking ourselves some tough questions about our lives, our world, our way of life. What would happen in our world if increasing numbers of us were to practice living this way? What would happen in our individual lives if we didn't just hear Jesus' words, if we didn't simply say "Lord, Lord!" but rather heard his words and acted on them? And what future might we predict for ourselves, our nation, and our planet if we reject Jesus' ethical manifesto in practice (even if we pay lip service to it in theory)?

—

CHAPTER 16

THE LANGUAGE OF THE KINGDOM

With what can we compare the kingdom of God,
or what parable shall we use for it?
—MARK 4:30 ESV

We've gone back and tried to imaginatively enter the time of Jesus so we can understand his secret message in its native habitat. But we can't stay back in ancient Israel. Jesus' message, as we've seen, is profoundly translatable. How would it translate into our world today?

As soon as we raise this question, we realize we have a problem—a major problem. As we've seen, when Jesus spoke of the kingdom of God, his language was charged with urgent political, religious, and cultural electricity. But today, if we speak of the kingdom of God, the original electricity is largely gone, and in its place we too often find a kind of tired familiarity that inspires not hope and excitement but rather anxiety or boredom.

Why is kingdom language not as dynamic today? First, because in our world, kingdoms are a thing of the past. They've given way to republics and democracies and democratic republics.

Now, authority resides in constitutions and parliaments and congresses. Where kings exist, they are by and large anachronisms, playing a limited ceremonial role in relation to parliaments and prime ministers, evoking nothing of the power and authority they did in Jesus' day. When people hear "kingdom of God," we don't want them to think "the anachronistic, limited, ceremonial, and symbolic but practically ineffectual rule of God"! If there is any electric charge to the language of kingdom today, it is the faint current of the quaint and nostalgic, conjuring knights in shining armor, round tables and chivalry, damsels in distress, fire-breathing dragons, and Shakespearean *thees* and *thous* that doth go running *hitherest* and *witherest*. In Jesus' day, kingdom language was contemporary and relevant; today, it is outdated and distant.

In addition, for many people today, kingdom language evokes patriarchy, chauvinism, imperialism, domination, and a regime without freedom. Not a pretty picture—and the very opposite of the liberating, barrier-breaking, domination-shattering, reconciling movement the kingdom of God was intended to be! So for these and other reasons, if Jesus were here today, I am quite certain he wouldn't use the language of kingdom *at all* . . . which leaves us wondering how he would in fact articulate his message today.

That's not simply a theoretical matter; it's a very practical question for people like me who believe that the secret message of Jesus has radical transformational potential today—and who feel called to try to communicate it. Of course, we will always need to go back to Jesus' original words and story, seeking to understand how kingdom language worked in his own day. We will always need to let his world "absorb" us so we can understand his kingdom language as insiders. But then we must discover fresh ways of translating his message into the thought forms and cultures of our contemporary world, if we are to "teach what Jesus taught in the manner he taught it."[1]

The search for the best translation is an artistic pursuit as well as a theological one. It involves not just a deep understanding of Jesus' message but also a substantial understanding of our contemporary culture and its many currents and crosscurrents. Whatever metaphors we choose will likely have a limited shelf life, and each will be open to various misunderstandings—just as Jesus' own metaphors were (which is why he would need to say things like, "My kingdom is not of this world"—necessary because some would misunderstand him to be organizing a new violent political regime).

I've been working and playing with a number of new (and used) metaphors for the last few years that seem to me to have some promise. I've had to drop a few for various reasons. For example, although Salvation Army founder William Booth used military metaphors to convey the kingdom of God, I believe that nuclear, biological, and chemical weapons—not to mention terrorism and imperialism—have made such language nearly unusable today. Similarly, *the global economy of God* might have potential—but not when it is seen as an expression of consumerism or materialism.

Six metaphors of the secret message strike me as having special promise.

1. *The dream of God.* I frequently try to put the prayer of the kingdom (what we often call "The Lord's Prayer") into my own words so that I don't just recite it on autopilot, saying the words without really considering what I'm saying. But I often struggle with how to paraphrase the clause "your will be done on earth as it is in heaven." This line of the prayer is especially important because—to put it grammatically—it is an appositive (the opposite of the opposite) to the clause "your kingdom come," meaning it is another way of saying the same thing. So this clause itself translates "kingdom" into "will."

But "the will of God" can evoke the idea of a despot, a tyrant, a puppeteer, a deterministic machine operator imposing his will, turning a prayer for liberation into a plea for an end to free will. (Of course, if God were such a controlling God, it's hard to imagine how such a prayer would ever become necessary in the first place!) Since the language of "will" can take us down a trail of control, domination, and coercion, and since I don't believe those ideas are in Jesus' mind at all, I have looked for other words.

The Greek word that lies beneath our English word *will* can also be translated *wish*. But to say, "May your wish come true" sounds rather fairy tale–ish and creates other problems. But I have found the idea of "the dream of God for creation" does the job quite nicely. "Your kingdom come, your will be done on earth as it is in heaven" could thus be rendered "May all your dreams for your creation come true." This language suggests a more personal, less mechanistic relationship between God and our world. It would resonate, for example, with a mother who has great dreams for her child, or a coach who has great dreams for her team, or an artist who has great dreams for a novel or painting or symphony he is creating, or a teacher who has high dreams for his students.

It also gives us language to talk about evil and sin in the world: these are nightmares for God. In creating our world, God wasn't dreaming of prisons and kidnapping, child abuse and racism, greed and poverty, pollution and exploitation, conformity and chaos. God's dream was for freedom and creativity, kindness and justice, generosity and peace, diversity and harmony.

This metaphor also gives us a responsible and creative role to play. If we dream of using or controlling others, raping the environment, ignoring the poor, perpetrating racism and other forms of injustice, or simply being lazy or selfish, we are ruining God's dream: our dreams are opposing God's dreams.

Recalling the five "moves" of chapter 13, the call to repentance is the call to rethink our dreams and realize their incompleteness or even destructiveness. The call to faith is the call to trust God and God's dreams enough to realign our dreams with God's, to dream our little dreams within God's big dream. The call to receptivity is the call to continually receive God's dreams—a process that, in my experience at least, seems to be a lifelong one. The call to baptism is the call to publicly identify with God's dream and to disassociate with all competing -isms or ideologies that claim to provide the ultimate dream (including nationalism, consumerism, hedonism, conservatism, liberalism, and so on). And the call to practice is the call to learn to live the way God dreams for us to live.

For all these reasons, "the dream of God" strikes me as a beautiful way to translate the message of the kingdom of God for hearers today. It is, of course, the language evoked by Dr. Martin Luther King Jr. as he stood on the steps of the Lincoln Memorial on August 28, 1963. His dream was God's dream, and that accounted for its amazing power.

2. *The revolution of God.* For people like Dr. King, attuned to fighting injustice, corruption, oppression, racism, and other forms of social evil, the *revolution* or *revolutionary movement* of God naturally flows from the metaphor of the dream of God for creation.

This metaphor claims that we human beings have created a totalitarian regime—a regime of lust (where too many people are reduced to sex objects or hyped into sexual predators), a regime of pride and power (where some thrive at the expense or to the exclusion of others), a regime of racism, classism, ageism, and nationalism (where people are identified as enemies or evil or inferior because of the color of their skin or the physical or social location of their birth), a regime of consumerism and greed (where life is commodified, where people become slaves to their jobs, where God's creation is reduced to natural resources for human consumption, where time is money, which makes life become money). This regime is unacceptable (an understatement, I hope you recognize), and God is recruiting people to join a revolutionary movement of change.

The revolution, of course, cannot use the corrupt tactics of the current regime; otherwise, it will only replace one corrupt regime with another. For example, if it uses violence to overcome violence, deceit to overcome deceit, coercion to overcome coercion, fear to overcome fear . . . then the revolution isn't really revolutionary; it's just a matter of lateral conversion or regime change. The very success of such a revolution would reinforce confidence in its tactics.

So perhaps we need a modifier in front of *revolution* to show how the goals and tactics of this regime are radically different: the peace revolution of God, the spiritual revolution of God, the love revolution of God, the reconciling revolution of God, the justice revolution of God. In these ways, we get much closer to the dynamic hidden in Jesus' original language of the kingdom of God.

My friends Dallas Willard and Tom Sine have used a related metaphor, speaking of the conspiracy of God (or "divine conspiracy" or "mustard seed conspiracy"). *Conspiracy* certainly resonates with the title of this book, suggesting secrecy, hiddenness. It is also rich with connotations—since the word means a group of people who speak in whispers and work so closely that they breathe one another's breath (*con* = with, *spir* = breath). God's conspiracy seeks to overturn the world as it is so that a new world can emerge.

3. *The mission of God.* The Latin term *missio Dei* has long been used to describe God's work in the world. Its etymology (*miss* = send) reminds us that God sends us into the world to be agents of change: we have a task to do for God. True, there is more to the kingdom than mission; being in relationship is essential to life in the kingdom, so kingdom life is not just doing work. But this

metaphor still has great value, as long as we complement it with more relational language too. (Actually, for some of us, it's collaboration in mission that creates the greatest relational connections.)

We might adapt the metaphor and speak of the medical mission of God, adding the relational connotations of caring and healing. Imagine that everyone on earth has become infected with a horrible virus. The virus makes people physically sick and mentally insane. Its symptoms vary from person to person and place to place: in one place it causes violence, in another sexual aggression, in another lying, in another paralysis, and so on.

Imagine that a doctor develops a cure. He brings the cure to you and says, "Once you take this medicine, you'll begin to feel better, but I'm not just giving you the cure for your sake. As soon as you feel well enough, I want you to make more of the cure and begin bringing it to others. And tell them the same thing: they are being healed not just so they can be healthy but also so they can become healers for the sake of others." Just as the disease spread "virally," now the cure will spread. A healing mission—where you are healed so you can join in healing others—would be an apt metaphor for the kingdom of God.

4. *The party of God.* Jesus often compared the kingdom to parties, feasts, and banquets. Today we could say that God is inviting people to leave their gang fights and come to a party, to leave their workaholism and rat race and come to a party, to leave their loneliness and isolation and join the party, to leave their exclusive parties (political ones, for example, which win elections by dividing electorates) and join one inclusive party of a different sort, to stop fighting or complaining or hating or competing and instead start partying and celebrating the goodness and love of God.

Just today I met some folks from a church in Minneapolis who demonstrate this metaphor in a dramatic and fun way. A group of them gather on a street corner in a poor part of town. They take overturned trash cans, old pots and pans, and an assortment of drums and other percussion instruments and start creating a loud, joyful rhythm. Soon a crowd gathers. It's impossible not to smile when you hear the joyful music being made mostly from junk. Homeless folk and people from the neighborhood start dancing. Then the church members start distributing food—not in the somber style of a soup kitchen, but in the joyful atmosphere of a street party. They don't have to say a word, really; they're demonstrating their message—that the kingdom of God is like a street party to which everybody is invited.

My friend Tony Campolo tells a true story that also serves as a great parable in this regard. He was in another time zone and couldn't sleep, so well after midnight he wandered down to a doughnut shop where, it turned out, local hookers also came at the end of a night of turning tricks. There, he overheard a conversation between two of them. One, named Agnes, said, "You know what? Tomorrow's my birthday. I'm gonna be thirty-nine." Her friend snapped back, "So what d'ya want from me? A birthday party? Huh? You want me to get a cake and sing happy birthday to you?" The first woman replied, "Aw, come on, why do you have to be so mean? Why do you have to put me down? I'm just sayin' it's my birthday. I don't want anything from you. I mean, why should I have a birthday party? I've never had a birthday party in my whole life. Why should I have one now?"

When they left, Tony got an idea. He asked the shop owner if Agnes came in every night, and when he replied in the affirmative, Tony invited him into a surprise party conspiracy. The shop owner's wife even got involved. Together they arranged for a cake, candles, and typical party decorations for Agnes, who was, to Tony, a complete stranger. The next night when she came in, they shouted, "Surprise!"—and Agnes couldn't believe her eyes. The doughnut shop patrons sang, and she began to cry so hard she could barely blow out the candles. When the time came to cut the cake, she asked if they'd mind if she didn't cut it, if she could bring it home—just to keep it for a while and savor the moment. So she left, carrying her cake like a treasure.

Tony led the guests in a prayer for Agnes, after which the shop owner told Tony he didn't realize Tony was a preacher. He asked what kind of church Tony came from, and Tony replied, "I belong to a church that throws birthday parties for prostitutes at 3:30 in the morning." The shop owner couldn't believe him. "No you don't. There ain't no church like that. If there was, I'd join it. Yep, I'd join a church like that." Sadly, there *are* too few churches like that, but if more of us understand the secret message of Jesus, there will be lots more.

5. *The network of God.* A promising new metaphor works with the idea of a network or system. God is inviting people into a life-giving network. First, God wants people to be connected, plugged in, in communication with God, so God can transfer to them what they need—not just information but also virus-debugging software, along with love, hope, empowerment, purpose, and wisdom. Also, each person who is connected to God must become integrally connected to all others in the network. In this way, the network of God breaks down the walls of smaller, exclusive networks (like networks of racism, nationalism, and the like) and invites them into the only truly world wide web of love. The network exchanges information and increases understanding for all participants. The network becomes a resource for people outside the network as well, and of course, people are always invited to enter the connectivity themselves.

The metaphor of an ecosystem could work in a similar way: we are currently living in an imbalanced, self-destructive ecosystem, but God is inviting us to live in a new network of relationships that will produce balance, harmony, and health. The metaphor of a community works along similar lines. One thinks of theologian Stanley Grenz speaking in terms of *the community of God*, or Dr. King's preferred phrases, *the beloved community* or *the inescapable network of mutuality*.[2]

6. *The dance of God.* In the early church, one of the most powerful images used for the Trinity was the image of a dance of mutual indwelling. The Father, Son, and Spirit live in an eternal, joyful, vibrant dance of love and honor, rhythm and harmony, grace and beauty, giving and receiving. The universe was created to be an expression and extension of the dance of God—so all creatures share in the dynamic joy of movement, love, vitality, harmony, and celebration. Electrons, protons, and neutrons—light, gravity, and motion—galaxies, suns, and planets—water, snow, ice, and vapor—winter, spring, summer, and fall—plants and animals, male and female—nations, tribes, clans, families, and individuals—art, sport, business, government, science, agriculture—every facet of creation had a role in the dance. But we humans broke with the dance. We stomped on the toes of other dancers, ignored the rhythm, rejected the grace, and generally made a mess of things. But God sent Jesus into the world to model for us a way of living in the rhythm of God's music of love, and ever since, people have been attracted to the beauty of his steps and have begun rejoining the dance.[3]

There are many other possible metaphors we could explore. We could talk about the inclusive tribe of God, for example: in a world of increasing tribalism, continually threatened by intertribal warfare and genocide, God is creating a barrier-breaking tribe that welcomes, appreciates, and links all tribes. This inclusive tribe isn't an in-group that makes other tribes into outgroups; rather, it's a "come on in" group that seeks to help all tribes maintain their unique identity and heritage while being invited into a tribe of tribes who live together in mutual respect, harmony, and love—because God is the universal tribal chief who created and loves all tribes.

Or we could talk about the story of God that invites people to become good characters, or the school of God that invites people to become students and then student teachers and then teachers, or the guild of God that invites people to learn the art of living from the Master. We could imagine the symphony or choir of God in which all of us can play or sing our unique parts with our unique voices. We can consider the team of God that invites us into training. Or we could talk about the friendship of God or the table of God or the invasion of God or the counter-insurgency of God or other possibilities that I haven't thought of but that you might—images of welcoming more and more people into an interactive relationship with God and all of creation.

In a sense, Jesus' creative use of parables sets an example for us to follow. It inspires us to ongoing creative communication—seeking to convey the kingdom through the symbolism of words as he did in the short fictional form of parable, and also in poetry, short story, novel, or essay. But it doesn't stop with the symbolism of words. People have been inspired to express the kingdom through the symbols of space and form, color and texture—in architecture and interior design. They have used the symbolism of movement and gesture in dance and drama. They've used the visual languages of painting and sculpture and collage and flower arranging and gardening. Even the symbolic language of taste can express the kingdom in cooking. Come to think of it, we might say that the kingdom of God is like an arts colony . . .

CHAPTER 17

THE PEACEABLE KINGDOM

The kingdom of heaven has suffered violence,
and the violent take it by force.
—Matthew 11:12 ESV

When we think of the language of Jesus' secret message, we realize quickly that for many people these days, to mix a political term like *kingdom* with a religious term like *God* sounds . . . scary, even terrorizing. We can't help but think of the dangerous religious-political cocktails of crusade and jihad, colonialism and terrorism, inquisition and fatwa—manifested in oxymoronic terms like *holy war* and *redemptive violence*. These intoxicating cocktails seem to uncheck humanity's darkest inhibitions so those who swallow them seek victory on their own terms, requiring from others submission, compliance, secrecy, or death. Their power-drunk arrogance is buttressed by absolute confidence—incapable of a second thought—that God is on their side.

In contrast, the kingdom that Jesus portrays exercises its power not in redemptive violence but in courageous, self-giving

love, and its goal is not victory on its own terms but rather peace
on God's terms. That peace—that *shalom*—means far more than
an end to conflict; it evokes a balanced and integrated "life to the
full." Jesus speaks on many occasions about his radically different
approach to power—an approach that deconstructs dominance
patterns in religion, family, education, and government (Matthew
23:1–12; Luke 22:24–27; John 13:1–15) and sees greatness in
service instead of in domination. With this radically fresh approach
to power in mind, we can't help but ask what the secret message
of Jesus has to say about violence and war. The subject is complex
and terribly important; the only thing worse than devoting a single chapter to it would be devoting none at all.[1]

Interestingly, Jesus' forerunner, John the Baptist—his opening act, so to speak—was asked a question very relevant to this
question of war. John called the people to a radical rethinking
(repentance) and told them they must produce fruit in line with
that repentance (Luke 3:8). People wanted to know what kind of
fruit he had in mind. He responded, "The person with two coats
and extra food should share with the person who has no coat or
food at all" (see v. 11). Then some soldiers came and asked what
they specifically should do.

Assuming that these were Jewish people who were working
for the Roman occupying army, their question is quite provocative. Would John say, "Go AWOL! Don't work for those violent
Romans! Be a pacifist instead!"? His answer is strong, but not
what we might expect: "Don't extort money and don't accuse
people falsely—be content with your pay" (v. 14).

In other words, he says, "Being a soldier gives you extraordinary
power. Don't abuse that power by extorting money or falsely
accusing people." Through Christian history, most Christians
have chosen to take a similar approach regarding war. It's not that
Christians should be pacifists, they say, but we shouldn't abuse

power—including the power of weaponry. We may still have to go to war, but we should be just and restrained in the way we conduct ourselves.

Others, though, have not been satisfied with this approach. They have looked at Jesus' kingdom manifesto, and they have felt it is impossible for a person to simultaneously put Jesus' teachings into action and participate in war. Leaders in the early church certainly followed this approach. Lee Camp summarizes their position, recalling Tertullian (born about AD 160), an early Christian leader:

> Confessing "Jesus is Lord" means taking Jesus seriously as Lord, as the authority for the believer: Caesar commands us to kill our enemies, and Jesus commands us to love them. Caesar makes use of torture and chains; Jesus calls us to forgiveness and holiness. So Tertullian asked:
>
> > Shall it be held lawful to make an occupation of the sword, when the Lord proclaims he who uses the sword shall perish by the sword? And shall the son of peace take part in the battle when it does not become him even to sue at law? And shall he apply the chain, and the prison, and the torture, and the punishment, who is not the avenger even of his own wrongs?[2]

There is much to commend this position. Jesus' apostles never once urge violence. Rather, they urge their followers to suffer, forgive, and trust God for the outcome rather than taking matters into their own hands. True, they talk about warfare and fighting, but not using conventional weapons. Consider these words from Paul—himself formerly a violent man who had not been squeamish about using violence in the service of God, as he formerly understood God. Paul asserts his authority, based not on the force of rhetoric, the power of position, or the coercion of weaponry:

> By the meekness and gentleness of Christ, I appeal to you. . . . [We do not] live by the standards of this world. For though we live in the world, we do not wage war as the world does. The weapons we fight with are not the weapons of the world. On the contrary, they have divine power to demolish strongholds. We demolish arguments and every pretension that sets itself up against the knowledge of God, and we take captive every thought to make it obedient to Christ. (2 Corinthians 10:1–5)

Elsewhere, Paul speaks of a similar arsenal of weapons not of the world. They are intended to fight "not against flesh and blood" but against "the authorities, against the powers of this dark world and against the spiritual forces of evil in the heavenly realms" (Ephesians 6:12). These weapons include the belt of truth, the breastplate of justice, the boots of the gospel of peace, the shield of faith, the helmet of salvation, and the sword of the Spirit—which he identifies with the logic (or message or *logos*) of God.

The crucifixion of Christ can in this light be seen as a radical repudiation of the use of violent force. As we've seen, the cross was the Roman tool of execution; it was reserved especially for leaders of rebellions. Anyone proclaiming a rival kingdom to the kingdom of Caesar would be a prime candidate for crucifixion. This is exactly what Jesus proclaimed, and this is exactly what he suffered—in between two others who had done the same. (The two men commonly thought of as thieves who were crucified with Jesus were more likely leaders or agents of failed political rebellions.) As we've seen, the *Pax Romana* was a peace made possible by the cross: people so feared crucifixion that they would think long and hard before rising up against the emperor.

It's stunning in this light that the church chose the cross as one of its primary symbols. What could choosing such an instrument of torture, domination, fear, intimidation, and death possibly mean?

For the early church, it apparently meant that the kingdom of God would triumph not by inflicting violence but by enduring it—not by making others suffer but by willingly enduring suffering for the sake of justice—not by coercing or humiliating others but by enduring their humiliation with gentle dignity. (This theme of enduring suffering is far more common in the teaching of Jesus and the apostles than most of us realize.) Jesus, they felt, took the empire's instrument of torture and transformed it into God's symbol of the repudiation of violence—encoding a creed that love, not violence, is the most powerful force in the universe.

It's no surprise in this light that the heroes of the early church were not Crusaders, not warriors, not men of the sword but rather martyrs, men and women with the faith and courage to face lion, ax, cross, chain, whip, and fire as testimony to their allegiance—not to the standards of this world but to the standards of the kingdom of God. Like Jesus, they would rather suffer violence than inflict it. Like Jesus, they showed that threats of violence could not buy their silence, that instruments of fear could not make them cower.

This orientation quickly changed when the Roman emperor Constantine claimed to convert to Christianity in the early fourth century. The Christian faith had gone from being an unknown religion to a misunderstood religion, to a persecuted religion, to a tolerated religion, to a favored religion, to the official religion of the Roman Empire. Gradually, Christians felt themselves protected by Rome's swords, not threatened by them. It grew harder and harder to criticize or distrust something that contributed to their own feeling of security. Eventually—this is hard to imagine, but the full truth of it must be faced—the church itself used the sword to force conversions and execute heretics. In fact, some of the cruelest tortures in the history of inhumanity were employed in the torture of those who were called heretics. (Whether the torturers were greater heretics by their very belief in torture is a question all should ponder.)

It's nightmarish to consider this: that the very language of "kingdom of God" would eventually be co-opted by leaders of the failing Roman regime and their successors to legitimize their use of violence in the name of Jesus Christ. It is nothing short of nauseating to ponder the fact that the symbol of the cross itself could be used by Christians just as it had been used by the Romans, painted on their shields as a way of saying, "Fear us! Resist us and we will kill you!" But the nauseating nightmare happened—and it continued for centuries, from the Crusades to witch trials to heretic burnings to KKK cross burnings. And it continues today in subtle ways many of us are hardly aware of.

In ten thousand heartbreaking ways, the secret message of Christ has been mocked by the behavior of those of us who bear his name. This is why we must ask ourselves the hard questions: Was the message of the kingdom of God intended to cause more religious wars, or was it actually a nonviolent alternative to war itself? Was it another violent movement or a movement against violence itself? Martin Luther King Jr. seemed to understand what was at stake as well as anyone, as this quote makes clear:

> Through violence you may murder a murderer, but you can't murder murder.
> Through violence you may murder a liar, but you can't establish truth.
> Through violence you may murder a hater, but you can't murder hate.
> Darkness cannot put out darkness. Only light can do that.[3]

Christians developed the "just war theory" in an attempt to grapple with the secret message of Jesus in the era after Constantine. Perhaps, St. Augustine thought, a Christian could not take up arms to defend himself, but shouldn't he do so to protect his neighbor? Wouldn't it be irresponsible not to do so?

The just war theory gave seven criteria for a "just war": a just cause for the war, a legitimate authority declaring war, a formal declaration of war, the goal being a return to peace, recourse to war only as a last resort, a reasonable hope of success, and means proportional to ends. The theory also presented three conditions for the prosecution of any war that met the seven criteria: noncombatants must not be targeted, prisoners must not be treated with cruelty, and international treaties and conventions must be respected. In this way, just war theory sought to balance competing demands: commitment to nonviolence in the way of Jesus and responsibility to protect neighbors from violence in the way of Jesus.

However we choose to integrate these competing demands, three things seem clear. First, those committed to nonviolence based on the teaching of Jesus—if they are wrong now—will someday be right. If God's dream is to come true for planet Earth, someday we will not "learn war anymore" (Isaiah 2:4 ESV). If we disagree with people presently committed to nonviolence, we should at least appreciate them for their foresight—just as we might look back and appreciate the earliest abolitionists, who believed slavery's days were numbered while their neighbors assumed that slavery would always be with us. Rather than saying they're wrong, we should say that they're ahead of their time—and that's not exactly a fault of theirs but of the times.

Second, in times of conflict, whenever we are tempted to label someone as "enemy" or "evil," we must remember Jesus' climactic words in his kingdom manifesto—that enemies are to be loved. They are to be loved not because it makes sense and not because it's a good security strategy, but because God blesses the evil and good alike with rain, and we are to imitate our King— not the kings of this world—as citizens in God's kingdom. Our love must rise above conventional levels (love your friends; hate your enemies) to imitate the expansive, boundary-crossing, merciful, and compassionate love of God. Otherwise, we only follow "the righteousness of the scribes and Pharisees"—*and we might as well admit it.*

Third, as one of Jesus' apostles said, we need to realize that both our enemies and we ourselves have a common enemy: the very internal darkness Jesus' secret message addresses—the dark drives of lust, greed, anger, and hate that thrust us into conflict and war (identified in the kingdom manifesto and echoed in James 4:1–3). We can't simply point out these splinters in our brothers' eyes in this regard; we must—in obedience to Jesus' kingdom manifesto—realize they distort our own vision too. Every warring nation emphasizes the evil of its enemy; few resist the temptation to minimize their own evil. Fewer still realize that the same evils are at work in both "them" and "us," and therefore pose a common, universal enemy—and it is this universal enemy that the kingdom of God fights with its weapons "not of this world."

The secret message of Jesus, by dealing with the root causes of war in this way, does not promise the easiest, fastest, safest, and most convenient method of ending violent conflict—but it offers, I believe, the only sure one. Perhaps as few people today will be willing to believe and practice this message as when it was first proclaimed. There are plenty of popular escape hatches for those who don't want to go there. But perhaps nearly two thousand years of trying these alternatives begin to make us ready to consider that Jesus may have been more right, more practical, and wiser than we realized, and his secret message may have meant what it said about loving—not killing—enemies.

We can all agree that so-called just war theory is better than unjust war theory. But we must ask if there is something better still. After all, it is certain that there has never been a so-called just war that did not create unjust consequences for thousands if not millions. And it is certain that there has never been a planned war that was canceled because it didn't meet the requirements of the theory. So perhaps it should no longer be called "just war theory" and instead be called, as Walter Wink has recommended, "preliminary violence reduction theory."

And perhaps we can agree that "preliminary violence reduction theory" is not the ultimate goal of the kingdom. Even though it is a better alternative than unconstrained violence, it must eventually give way to the best alternative of all, which is the focus of Jesus' secret message. When Jesus said, "Blessed are the peacemakers," when he spoke of turning the other cheek, walking the second mile, and giving freely, he was telling us that *active peacemaking* is the best way—the way of the kingdom. Again, listen to Dr. King:

Peace is not merely a distant goal that we seek, but a means by which we arrive at that goal. . . . We will not build a peaceful world by following a negative path. It is not enough to say "we must not wage war." It is necessary to love peace and sacrifice for it. We must concentrate not merely on the negative expulsion of war but the positive affirmation of peace. . . . We must see that peace represents a sweeter music, a cosmic melody, that is far superior to the discords of war.

Somehow, we must transform the dynamics of the world power struggle from the negative nuclear arms race, which no one can win, to a positive contest to harness humanity's creative genius for the purpose of making peace and prosperity a reality for all the nations of the world. In short, we must shift the arms race into a "peace race." If we have a will and determination to mount such a peace offensive, we will unlock hitherto tightly sealed doors of hope and bring new light into the dark chambers of pessimism.[4]

I refuse to accept the view that mankind is so tragically bound to the starless midnight of racism and war that the bright daybreak of peace and brotherhood can never become reality. I believe that unarmed truth and unconditional love will have the final word.[5]

To me, these words from Dr. King echo the "unarmed truth" of the secret message of Jesus far more than the words of those who say Jesus' message is not relevant, or at least not now.

I write during a time of war, and one can't address this issue as I have without people wondering if this approach will lead to a dishonoring of the soldiers and their families who make such great sacrifices from which the rest of us derive benefit. It is easy indeed to slip to one extreme or the other—vilifying all things military on the one hand or praising all things military on the other. The secret message of Jesus, I suggest, calls us to a more difficult third way. First, we must assert that the kingdom of God never advances *by* or *through* war or violence. Yes, the kingdoms of this world frequently do so advance, temporarily at least (although we must remember Jesus' words that those who live by the sword will also die by it). But we can never claim that the anger of humanity accomplishes the righteousness (or justice) of God, as James said (1:20), nor that the violence of humanity accomplishes the kingdom of God.

Second, we must add this: that even though the kingdom does not advance through violence, it may advance *during times* or *episodes* of violence. Where violence occurs, we should expect

God's love to be gathering, like antibodies around a pathogen, to bring healing. And perhaps we can extend the metaphor further: perhaps each time the disease of violence infects us, the kingdom of God is at work to build immunity against the next infection.

That's why I believe that we are often better off having people who have a vision for God's kingdom serving in the military than not having them there. Whether they're chaplains, technicians, strategists, commanders, or soldiers, *they know* that there is a higher standard than national interest or expediency, and they seek to live by that higher standard, even when doing so requires great courage and sacrifice. Some people may forget that the enemy is beloved by God and is in fact their neighbor, but those with a vision of the kingdom of God can't forget.

Of course, this knowledge won't make their lives easier. There will be times and situations where agents of the kingdom will not be able to serve or obey orders as others might: a con-science informed by the secret message of Jesus will forbid them.[6] In the best of times, agents of the kingdom will face unique difficulties and challenges—but so do we all, whether we're in business, government, art, science, the trades, or even ministry. There are business deals that can't be made, or products that shouldn't be manufactured or sold or advertised, or movie scripts that aren't worth acting in or directing, or campaigns that people of kingdom-conscience must drop out of. And in their place, there are initiatives for peace and justice in which people of the kingdom must actively participate, whatever the cost.

This approach becomes all the more necessary, I believe, when we realize that the twentieth-century creation of nuclear, biological, and chemical weapons puts the just war theory into question. Can the criteria of just war be met when virtually any conflict might spin out of control and into nuclear catastrophe, or the unleashing of uncontrollable disease, or the spread of clouds of deadly gases that kill every living thing they touch? Never before the late modern era have humans had the potential to wipe out all life on the planet. That new power—with its unimaginable capacity for abuse—is reason enough for us to reconsider whether it is time, in light of the secret message of Jesus, to move beyond preliminary violence reduction theory as our high-water mark, and instead set our sights on an even better way: the way of vigorous, enthusiastic, hopeful, passionate, active peacemaking—making "sustained, concerted attempts to institutionalize means of preventing war."[7]

It is time, I believe, for people who have confidence in Jesus and his message to lead the way in imagining what could happen—say over ten or twenty or a hundred years—if increasing percentages of our budgets were diverted from peacekeeping through weaponry to peacemaking through actively addressing the underlying causes of conflict—causes like injustice, lack of compassion, racism, corruption, lack of free and ethical press, and poverty—and the fear, hatred, greed, ignorance, and lust that fuel them. Either way, the cost will be high; it's just a question of which kind of cost we would prefer to pay.

If people believe that wars are necessary and justified, then wars will continue to happen. If people believe in redemptive violence, then violence will proliferate. But if they believe the secret message of Jesus, they will believe that there are creative alternatives to war and violence, and by the grace of God, fewer and fewer wars and less and less violence may happen as a result. And someday, by the grace of God, perhaps war will go the way of slavery and colonialism—so that we can say that the kingdom of God has more fully come.[8]

In the meantime, the word of John the Baptist should be heard by everyone who has power: "Repent and bring forth fruits of your repentance!" (see Luke 3:8). Soldiers, politicians, military strategists, weapons manufacturers, and taxpayers who pay their salaries may ask, "What about us? What should we do?" Journalists, news directors, TV and radio anchors and reporters, and bloggers would join them: "What about us? What should we do?"

John the Baptist would answer, I believe, just as he did back in the months before Jesus emerged on the scene: "Don't abuse your power. And listen to the one whose way I was sent to prepare. He will take away the sin of the world."

Whether we're presently pacifists or supporters of preliminary violence reduction theory, whenever we pray, "Your kingdom come; your will be done on earth as it is in heaven," we're praying that war and violence will end and God's *shalom* will come. That in itself is an act of peacemaking, because we're seeking to align our wills with God's will, our dreams with God's dream.

CHAPTER 18

THE BORDERS OF
THE KINGDOM

Woe to you, teachers of the law and Pharisees, you hypocrites! You shut the door of the kingdom of heaven in people's faces. You yourselves do not enter, nor will you let those enter who are trying to.

—MATTHEW 23:13 TNIV

Early on in my exploration of Jesus' secret message, it became clear to me that the exclusive attitude of the Pharisees and religious scholars angered Jesus. In ways that were sure to infuriate them in return, he loved to compare the kingdom of God to a party. He would demonstrate the open border of the kingdom of God by hosting or participating in parties where even the most notorious outcasts and sinners were welcome.

Jesus was often criticized for this "table fellowship" with notorious sinners; his critics assumed that Jesus' acceptance of these people implied an approval and endorsement of their shabby behavior. But they misunderstood: Jesus wanted to help them experience transformation. Rejection hardens people, but acceptance makes transformation possible. By accepting and welcoming people into his presence, just as they were, with all their problems and imperfections, Jesus was exposing them to his example and to his secret message. In this way, he could challenge them to think—and think again—and consider becoming part of the kingdom of God so they could experience and participate in the transformation that flows from being in interactive relationship with God and others.[1]

But Jesus' wide acceptance of people seems to be in tension with a number of his statements that have an exclusive ring of their own. For example, "To you has been given the secret of the kingdom of God, but for those outside, everything comes in parables" (Mark 4:11 NRSV). So we are left to wonder, does the kingdom of God include everybody as insiders, or does it leave some on the outside?

Again, the thrust of Jesus' message is about inclusion—shocking, scandalous inclusion: *the kingdom of God is available to all, beginning with the least.*[2] Yet Jesus often warns people of the possibility of missing the kingdom. "Unless you become like a little child," he said, "you shall not enter the kingdom" (see Matthew 18:3). So the possibility is real: the kingdom of God that is available to all can be missed by some.

This concern is especially relevant these days when the Christian religion is too often perceived as a divisive, judgmental, rancorous, and exclusionary movement—nearly the opposite of a kingdom of peace, available to all, beginning with the least. How can some people interpret Jesus' message as exclusive, while others see it as the most radically inclusive message in human history? What is the truth about Jesus' message: Is it, like most religious messages, about in-groups and out-groups, us versus them, condemnation and exclusion? Or is it indeed an embracing message with good news for all people? Can any meaningful kingdom, including the kingdom of God, exist with no boundaries, no outside?

Before you say yes, ask yourself this question: Does the kingdom of God say, "You are forced to be in whether you want to be or not? There is no escape. You will be assimilated"? That doesn't sound like freedom. It sounds like conquest.

Echoing Jesus' method, let's create a parable.

Once there was a sheep farmer. He had a high fence around his property to protect his sheep from wolves. But then one handsome young buck said, "Why are we so exclusive around here? Everyone knows that sheep are peaceful creatures, but to have this wall up around us makes it seem like we're fearful, exclusive elitists." So they rammed the fence posts with their heads until the fence posts toppled and a breach was open in the fence.

Soon a band of wolves passed by. Their leader said, "We would be idiots to rush in and start eating sheep in broad daylight. The sheep would panic, and the fence would be rebuilt. Let's move in among them and pretend to be their friends, and we can eat well for years to come." He approached the leader of the sheep and said, "We see your goodwill gesture, and we would like to live among you in peace." The sheep were pleased. Their peace strategy had worked! Day after day, wolves and sheep would lie down in the sun, enjoying the green pastures. The wolves would even eat a few mouthfuls of grass to reassure the sheep that they weren't a threat at all.

But each night, the wolves would find a sheep that had drifted away from the herd and have a feast. The next morning, when the sheep would realize one of their number was missing, the wolves would pretend to be outraged and would join them in a pretend search for the perpetrators. Eventually the sheep realized they had been tricked, and they asked the farmer to rebuild the fence, and they became more distrustful of outsiders than they had been before.

It's clear: the judgmentalism and exclusion that are often associated with religion are a terrible problem in our world. But it's also true that saying, "Everybody's in, everybody's fine, everybody's an insider" doesn't solve all the problems either; it creates new ones.

So we come to realize that there is not one set of dangers, there are two: dangers of hostile exclusion and dangers of naive inclusion. You can't solve one problem simply by going to its opposite; there has to be a third way that is different from both permissive, naive inclusiveness and hostile, distrustful exclusion. How does the secret message of Jesus deal with this dual problem?

We've seen in the secret message of Jesus that God's kingdom extends a scandalously open invitation. As we've seen, it doesn't begin with the greatest—the "righteous," the healthy, the wealthy, the aggressive, or the wise. It begins with the least—the sinners, the sick, the poor, the meek, and the children. Entry isn't on the basis of merit, achievement, or superiority, but rather it requires humility to think again, to become teachable (like a child), and to receive God's forgiveness and reconciling grace (like a runaway child returning home and being joyfully welcomed).

So, returning to our parable, we need a third option. A high fence that excludes everyone won't do, nor will no fence at all. What we need is a requirement that those who wish to enter actually have a change of heart—that they don't sneak in to accomplish their own agenda, but rather that they genuinely want to learn a new way of thinking, feeling, living, and being in "the pastures of God." Perhaps that is why baptism—a ritual washing indicating repentance and a desire to begin again—was so important to Jesus' predecessor, John the Baptist; to Jesus and his disciples; and to the apostles who followed them. It was important to call people to a change of heart and give them a dramatic way of going public by saying, "Yes, this change of heart has happened within me, and I'm willing to identify myself publicly as a person who is on a new path." And perhaps the Christian ritual of Eucharist was intended to function in a similar way—a kind of regular recommitment where people say, by gathering around a table and sharing in bread and wine, that they are continuing Jesus' tradition of gathering in an inclusive community. "I'm still in," they're saying. "My heart is still in this mission and dream. I'm still committed."

Let's test this idea by comparing it with other areas of life. If the kingdom of God were a symphony, it would welcome anyone who had a desire to learn to play music—from tuba players to piccolo players, from violinists to percussionists. It would accept beginners and master musicians, wisely pairing up the novices with mentors who could help them learn. But it could not welcome people who hated music or who wanted to shout and scream and disrupt rehearsals and concerts; that would ruin the music for everyone and destroy the symphony. True, it would try to influence music haters to become music lovers, but it couldn't accept them into the symphony until they wanted to be there because of a love for music.

If the kingdom of God were a soccer club, it could welcome children and adults, males and females, beginners and stars—but it couldn't welcome people who hated soccer and wanted to replace it with kickboxing.

If the kingdom of God were a hospital, it could accept sick people needing healing, doctors and nurses seeking to serve and cure people, and guests wanting to visit the sick. But it couldn't welcome people coming in to kidnap babies from the nursery, nor could it welcome phony doctors pretending to care only so they can inflict pain, nor could it welcome people intent on pulling out plugs in the intensive care unit.

The kingdom of God, then, seeks a third way: not exclusiveness and rejection on the one hand, and not foolish, self-sabotaging inclusion on the other hand, but rather *purposeful inclusion*. In other words, the kingdom of God seeks to include all who want to participate in and contribute to its purpose, but it cannot include those who oppose its purpose.

An enigmatic series of statements in episodes recorded by Luke (chapters 9–11) illustrates this idea of purposeful inclusion. In the first episode (9:46–48), Jesus' disciples are—stupidly but predictably—arguing about which of them will be considered the greatest. This is a classic case of creating boundaries to divide an exclusive in-group of "the greatest" from an out-group of everyone else. Jesus dramatically takes a child and stands him by his side and says that whoever in Jesus' name welcomes (or gladly includes) a little child—a person of no perceived social status or greatness—welcomes Jesus, and in fact welcomes God. Then he adds, "He who is least among you all—he is the greatest" (v. 48), effectively confounding any attempt to erect a ladder of status and domination to judge and exclude. The ladder is turned upside down!

Immediately, it seems, John understands the implications of what Jesus has just said. He reports that he and his fellow disciples recently saw someone casting out demons in Jesus' name, "and we tried to stop him, because he is not one of us" (v. 49). Again, this is classic boundary-erecting behavior of an exclusive in-group. Jesus replies, "Do not stop him, . . . for whoever is not against you is for you" (v. 50). In the space of a few minutes, Jesus twice rejects an exclusive in-group attitude among his followers and corrects them—first for seeking the exclusive status of greatness and then for opposing someone for not being "one of us."

But how do we relate this inclusive attitude—"whoever is not against you is for you"—with what Jesus says just two chapters later: "He who is not with me is against me, and he who does not gather with me, scatters" (11:23)? We might conclude that Jesus is contradicting himself—until we look at the context, where we see that here Jesus is in a very different situation. Now he is being accused by critics of doing miracles by satanic power. He responds that such an accusation is illogical: why would Satan oppose Satan? Then he adds, "Any kingdom divided against itself will be ruined" (11:17).

Seen in this context, Jesus' meaning begins to become clear. Just as a satanic kingdom would be ruined if its citizens were divided against one another, so God's kingdom would be ruined if its citizens were working at cross purposes. If people refuse to join *with* Jesus in his inclusive purpose of gathering, welcoming, reconciling, or uniting in God's kingdom, they will in fact be perpetuating the division, exclusion, or *scattering* that the kingdom has come to heal, and they will in this way be working *against* him.

Now we can make sense of both statements: "whoever is not against you is for you" argued against a narrow exclusion, and "he who is not with me is against me" argued against a naive inclusion. The kingdom's purpose is to gather, to include, to welcome everyone who is willing (children, prostitutes, tax collectors) into reconciliation with God and one another—but if the kingdom included people who rejected this purpose, the kingdom, "divided against itself," would be ruined. This purposeful inclusion is the better path, even though it isn't an easy one either to understand or to follow.

In so many of his parables and teachings and certainly in his daily life, it's clear that Jesus doesn't want us judging, out-grouping, trying to sift between wheat and chaff, or holding people at arm's distance. Yet in his repeated challenges to repent, to follow him, to learn his meekness and humility, he is making clear that citizens of the kingdom must indeed want to learn a new way of life, and if they don't count and pay the full cost, they will remain outside. You hear him making the cost clear in statements like, "Any of you who does not give up everything he has cannot be my disciple" (Luke 14:33) or, "No one who puts his hand to the plow and looks back is fit for service in the kingdom" (Luke 9:62).

No wonder this third way seems paradoxical: to be truly inclusive, the kingdom must exclude exclusive people; to be truly reconciling, the kingdom must not reconcile with those who refuse reconciliation; to achieve its purpose of gathering people, it must not gather those who scatter. The kingdom of God has a purpose, and that purpose isn't everyone's cup of tea.

Martin Luther King Jr. learned what happens when you preach an inclusive message of reconciliation. Bishop Romero learned what happens when you call people to gather rather than scatter. Desmond Tutu and Nelson Mandela learned what happens when you try to expand the borders of who is considered "in" and worthy of dignity and respect. On the one hand, if you start expanding the borders and working for a God-centered inclusive and reconciling network of relationships, you will quickly find that there are plenty of people willing to insult you, imprison you, torture you, and kill you. They prefer the rigid boundaries and impermeable walls of their narrow domains and constricted turf, not God's purposefully inclusive kingdom that calls the least "the greatest" and welcomes the outcast.

On the other hand, if you try to include those people who oppose your inclusive purpose, then your kingdom is divided against itself, and it will be ruined. So what do you do? If you're Jesus, you take whatever space you are given and let God's kingdom be made visible and real there. It might be a beach near a lake or a field near a hillside. It might be a home in a village. It might be on a boat, or along a road, or next to a well, or even in a temple or synagogue. You do what you can to make that space inclusive for all who want to experience the kingdom. You make that space an open border crossing, so to speak. And if critics see you as a transgressor and criticize you for opening the doors and expanding the boundaries, you go on pursuing your purpose, making it clear that the kingdom of God is open to all, except those who want to ruin it by dividing it against itself. But even they, if they have a change of heart, will be welcomed in.

CHAPTER 19

THE FUTURE OF
THE KINGDOM

*They asked him, "Lord, are you at this time going
to restore the kingdom to Israel?"*
—ACTS 1:6

"May your kingdom come. May your will be done on earth as it is in heaven," we pray. But when will our prayers be answered? The disciples asked the same question, just after the Resurrection. Jesus doesn't correct them as we might expect by telling them, "Wake up, you duh-sciples! It's already here!" or, "It won't come for more than 2,500 years, so stop asking!" Instead, he tells them it's none of their business to speculate about how God plans to work out history, and then he gives them a mission to accomplish. (That mission, it turns out, may actually be the answer to their question, since the kingdom of God isn't just a status: it's a mission and a story in which they—and we—can play a part.)

When *will* the kingdom fully come? And what should we expect between now and then—for things to get better and better, or worse and worse, or a mixture of both? If we're confused on the subject, in part the cause of our confusion no doubt relates to Jesus' rather baffling array of statements about the kingdom's coming. In some cases, it sounds like the fullness of the kingdom is still in the future: "I tell you the truth, some who are standing here will not taste death before they see the kingdom of God come with power" (Mark 9:1; cf. Matthew 16:28; Luke 9:27). "Nation will rise against nation, and kingdom against kingdom. . . . Even so, when you see these things happening, you know that the kingdom of God is near" (Luke 21:10, 31).

Yet in other places, Jesus uses the same phrase—"the kingdom of God is near"—clearly referring to the present time (Luke 10:9–11). And in a number of places, as we've seen, he makes it clear that he doesn't want people to speculate about the time frame for the coming of the kingdom at all.

Once, having been asked by the Pharisees when the kingdom of God would come, Jesus replied, "The coming of the kingdom of God is not coming with signs to be observed, nor will they say, 'Look, here it is!' or 'There!' for behold, the kingdom of God is in the midst of you" (Luke 17:20–21 ESV ["In the midst of you" may also be rendered "within you"]). Jesus responds in a similar way in Luke 19:11–17: "Because he was near Jerusalem and the people thought that the kingdom of God was going to appear at once," Jesus tells a parable that turns his hearers away from speculation about the future and instead focuses on their behavior here and now.

In spite of these warnings about speculation, some people believe that the Bible gives a clear timeline of the future, and they speculate with gusto about what the timeline is. They believe that history is, in some sense, like a movie that is already written, already directed or determined, in God's mind. It has already been filmed, edited, and put into the can, and we're just watching it play. The Bible gives them a code to know what to expect in the rest of the movie. People who take this approach don't necessarily agree on how to interpret the Bible in general or the teachings of Jesus in particular, but they at least agree that the future is already more or less determined.

Others—and I am among them, although I was born and thoroughly indoctrinated into the former approach—believe that neither the Bible nor the teachings of Jesus are intended to give us a timeline of the future. In our view, God intended to create our universe the way parents give birth to a child: the child is given limits and guidance, but she also has freedom to live her own life. That means that the future of the universe is not determined as if it were a movie that's already been filmed and is just being shown to us. Nor is it completely left to chance like dice cast on a table. Rather, God's creation is maturing with both freedom and limits under the watchful eye of a caring parent. So what we find in the Bible and the teachings of Jesus are not determining prognostications or schematic diagrams of the future but instead something far more valuable: warnings and promises.

Warnings tell us that if we make foolish or unjust choices, bad consequences will follow. Prophets from Moses to Jesus frequently give these kinds of warnings. Their purpose is not to tell the future but to change the future. In warning the people about future negative consequences of bad behavior, the prophet's greatest hope is that his predictions of calamity will not come true. He hopes that disaster will be averted by warning the people of disaster, much as a mother does when she warns her children who are throwing rocks, "You're having fun now, but somebody's going to lose an eye!" If the children understand her warning, they will stop throwing rocks, and nobody will lose an eye: this means that her warning has succeeded—even though what she "predicted" failed to happen. (This very thing happens in the book of Jonah in the Old Testament: the prophet predicts the destruction of Nineveh, the people of Nineveh repent, and they aren't destroyed. The irony, of course, is that Jonah is disappointed; he would have preferred the Ninevites to be incinerated!)

Promises also differ from prognostications. If I tell my children, "I'll always be there for you," I'm not making a prediction, because I will eventually die, and my statement won't be true. But taken as a promise, the statement is true. Or I might make a conditional promise: "Do your homework every day, and I will take you out to dinner." I'm not predicting what will happen. Rather, I'm promising that I will do something in my power—if my children do something within their power. My promise works with and intensifies their sense of empowerment.

Prognostications can have the opposite effect. If I predict, "You will fail no matter how hard you try," you will be less likely to try. You will feel despairing, stuck, and powerless. If I predict, "You will succeed even if you don't try," you may also be less likely to give your best effort or make heroic sacrifice. You will be tempted to laziness or complacency. So prognostications are rather tricky things.

People who read the warnings and promises of the Bible as prognostications have to figure out how to arrange the warnings and promises in chronological order.[1] So their schematics of the future might go warning-warning-promise-warning-promise, or promise-promise-warning-warning-warning-promise. They might say there will be an unknown length of time with promise, then seven years of warning, then a thousand years of promise, then another warning, then an eternity of promise. The possible arrangements are nearly endless.

But if we take the biblical material less as prognostications and more as promises and warnings for their original hearers, we have a much simpler scenario: we humans live with ever-present warning and promise, with the ultimate warning that evil and injustice will lose and the ultimate promise that God and good will win. The goal is not to place us in a fatalistic, determined universe that makes us succumb to can't-win disempowerment, fatalism, despair, and resignation—or can't-lose overconfidence, complacency, arrogance, and triumphalism. Instead, warnings and promises serve to heighten our sense of responsibility and accountability, and they wake us up—like children throwing rocks—to realize that serious consequences could flow from our current carelessness. If we believe the warnings and promises, we won't persist in doing evil or being complacent, but we will persist in doing good and being fruitful, even if it's hard.[2]

At this point, some readers will wonder about the book of Revelation, the last book in the Bible, which many people have read as a coded blueprint predicting the future. Let me offer this analogy to propose an alternative approach. If you've been to an old-fashioned zoo, you've seen a lion or elephant pacing a cement floor behind iron bars. If you stood at the rail of an old-fashioned zoo and watched the caged lion or elephant for a few years, you would learn certain things about it. But what you would learn would be miniscule compared to what you could learn if instead you went to Africa and watched lions and elephants in their natural environment over a few years. There, you would see their social lives, their sex lives, their hunting habits, and their migration patterns.

Similarly, if you put Revelation on a concrete slab behind iron bars, you will learn something, but you'll misunderstand its true nature unless you set it free in its natural habitat. What is its natural habitat? The book of Revelation is an example of a popular literary genre of ancient Judaism, known today as *Jewish apocalyptic*. Trying to read it without understanding its genre would be like watching *Star Trek* or some other science-fiction show thinking it was a historical documentary, or watching a sitcom as if it were a religious parable, or reading a satire as if it were a biography—or like thinking you knew all about lions because you watched one pacing on a concrete slab one afternoon.

But Jewish apocalyptic itself is part of a larger ecosystem known as *literature of the oppressed*. When you read Revelation first in its native niche of Jewish apocalyptic, and then in its native ecosystem of literature of the oppressed, it comes alive and you see it in a fresh way. Instead of being a book about the distant future, it becomes a way of talking about the challenges of the immediate present. It becomes a book of warnings and promises.[3]

The original readers of Revelation lived in constant threat of religious oppression from the religious authorities and the Roman Empire. In that environment, you can't speak—and certainly can't write—a word of criticism against the government and other authorities; if you are caught with such subversive literature in your possession, you'll be imprisoned, maybe killed. But if you don't speak or write about your oppression, your oppressors have succeeded in controlling you, silencing you, intimidating you. Is there any alternative? Yes, and this is the genius of literature of the oppressed in general and of apocalyptic literature in particular.

Here's what you do: you tell the truth about those in power—that they're corrupt, bloodthirsty, and doomed—but you do so covertly. You don't talk about the "Roman Empire"; you talk about the "Beast." You don't talk about the corrupt religious authorities; you personify them as a false prophet. You don't talk about the emperor; you tell a story about a dragon. In this way, you refuse to be silenced in fear—and you don't create incriminating evidence that could lead to torture and death for the author and readers of the literature.

If Revelation were a blueprint of the distant future, it would have been unintelligible for its original readers, as well as the readers of all succeeding generations, and would only become

truly and fully relevant for one generation—the one who happened to live in the one period of time it is prognosticating about.
But if Revelation is instead an example of the literature of the
oppressed, full of ever-relevant warnings and promises, it presents
each generation with needed inspiration and wisdom and encouragement. In this light, Revelation becomes a powerful book
about the kingdom of God here and now, available to all.

In its original context, the book of Revelation seems to say
something like this:

> Yes, the religious authorities and the Roman Empire are perse-
> cuting us. The emperor—the king of kings—thinks he is the
> ultimate authority. But we are part of the empire of God, the
> kingdom of God. Our King of kings will ultimately triumph.
> God's kingdom will last forever. The Roman emperor and the
> religious systems that collide with him will succumb to the
> forces of history, and the Roman Empire will run its course and
> eventually disintegrate. So let's remain faithful, even to death.
> Let's not be intimidated but rather be full of confidence and
> hope. Let's focus on the glorious reality of God's kingdom and
> see the current powers that be as a passing phenomenon.
> Instead of letting our imaginations be captivated by fearful
> scenes of torture and death, let's fill our imaginations with
> another vision of reality that will allow us to endure with joy.

To say these things overtly would have been treasonous. But
to say and read them in these covert ways would be courageous
and liberating.

Other readers will be thinking of long passages in the
Gospels that seem to be full of prognostication from the lips of
Jesus himself—prognostications that seem to relate to the end of
the world. What are we to make of these passages, such as

Matthew 24–25? This is a subject no less deep, complex, and contentious than interpreting Revelation, and in light of the thousands of books that have been written on the subject, it seems impossible to offer an alternative view in just a few paragraphs. Even so, let me sketch out this alternative approach briefly in hopes that you will explore it more deeply on your own.

Since Jewish apocalyptic was a popular genre in Jesus' day, we would expect him to be influenced by it and use its language and metaphors. If that is the case, we would need to approach Jesus' language about the future as we would the language of Revelation. So, against the backdrop of Jewish apocalyptic, we discover that phrases that sound like they're about the destruction of the world—like "the moon will turn to blood" or "the stars will fall from the sky"—are actually rather typical stock phrases in Jewish apocalyptic. They're no more to be taken literally than phrases we might read in the paper today: "The election results were earth-shattering." Or, "The president's announcement sent shock waves through Congress." Or, "On September 11, 2001, everything changed."

We can easily imagine someone thousands of years from now, armed with an English dictionary but without much experience reading newspapers, writing this interpretation: "People in the twenty-first century believed that natural phenomena were caused by political events. For example, they believed that an election or presidential announcement could cause a shift in plate tectonics, resulting in earthquakes and tremors. Or they believed a terrorist attack could create an ontological shift that would alter the fundamental nature of matter and energy, space and time." We may be stupid, but we're not that stupid—and similarly, Jesus and his contemporaries should not be presumed to believe that the moon would literally be turned into a mixture of white blood cells, red blood cells, and plasma or that huge stars, defying gravity, would actually converge on our tiny earth.

With this sensitivity, a very different picture emerges of Jesus' eschatological intentions. You'll remember the political back-drop we explored in the first chapters of this book: seething under the surface in the Jewish community was the question of how to respond to the Roman occupation, and two main kinds of answers arose, as Jay Gary brilliantly and simply explains in an article called "The Future According to Jesus."[4] First, there is a *conventional future* with the status quo continuing on uninterrupted. This future of collaboration, capitulation, and compromise is preferred by those who are enjoying and profiting from it: Sadducees and Herodians. Second, there are various *counterfutures* imagined by various groups for whom the status quo is not so profitable or satisfying. There is the *fight response* of the Zealots (fight, rebel, terrorize), the *flight response* of the Essenes (isolate, evacuate, escape), and the *blame response* of the Pharisees (con-demn, shame, avoid). Jesus enters with a *creative future*. He says, "Do not believe any of these people or follow them either in capitulation or in fight, flight, or blame. It is time to live in a rad-ically new way—the way of the kingdom of God. Learn from me how to take this path—it's the only way to avoid destruction."

What is the destruction that needs to be avoided—if it's not the end of the world? Jesus apparently foresees a scenario some-thing like this: "Tensions will continue to rise, and eventually the Zealots will lead the people into a violent rebellion. When they rebel, God will not intervene as they hope, because God does not want to continue to bless violence. Instead, they will be crushed brutally by the Romans. The temple will be destroyed. Jerusalem will fall. Jewish life as we know it will end."

If you read the Gospels in this light, I believe you will agree that Jesus' warnings come together in a coherent and satisfying way—far more coherent and satisfying than the conventional approaches. Yes, Jesus uses apocalyptic language that sounds like it's talking about the literal end of the world. But when we understand the way the genre works—when we interpret a sitcom as a sitcom, science fiction as science fiction, and opera as opera—we realize that Jesus is speaking pointedly, and in a way his contemporaries would understand, about concrete political realities.

And as anyone who knows history will realize, the scenario Jesus described did in fact occur. His countrymen did not trust him or follow him. They rejected both his promises and his warnings. They did not accept his radical alternative to violence, accommodation, or isolation. Jesus himself realizes this will be the case as he descends to Jerusalem on what we call Palm Sunday, and he begins to weep and says, "Jerusalem, Jerusalem! If only you knew what makes for peace!" Because they rejected his way, tensions did rise. The Zealots did stage a revolt in AD 67. The Romans did come in and crush Jerusalem and destroy the temple and wipe out the historic temple system of sacrifice. For the Jews of that day, the moon did turn to blood and the stars did fall from the sky—these events were truly (but not literally) "earth-shattering."

So then, what are we left with to say about the future, if the apocalyptic passages of the Gospels and of Revelation are not simply coded timelines of the future?[5] We are left with something far more powerful and important—we are left with a balance of promises and warnings, a sense of profound empowerment and responsibility, and a sobering choice.

If Jesus was right, if the kingdom of God has come and is coming in the ways we've described, if we do indeed have the choice today and every day to seek it, enter it, receive it, live as citizens of it, invest in it, even sacrifice and suffer for it . . . then today our future hangs in the balance no less than it did for Jesus' original hearers in AD 30 or so. We can invest in today's conventional futures or counterfutures, or we can seek the creative future offered by Jesus.

If we trust Jesus, if we follow his way, if we believe that the impossible is possible—in our personal and family affairs as well as in our public policy and international affairs—we will make decisions and choose directions of one sort. If we believe his way is unrealistic or too difficult or just plain stupid, we will make other decisions and choose other directions. It is not an over-statement to say of us and our generation what we could have said of Jesus own contemporaries: depending on how we respond to his secret message of the kingdom of God, we will create two very different worlds, two very different futures—one hellish, the other heavenly.

One world is all too familiar to us. It is a future too much like our past: full of regret and pain—which is exactly what hellish language like "weeping and gnashing of teeth" is intended to evoke. It is a world of increasing violence and disease, environ-mental degradation and economic disaster, division at every level of society, and on an individual level—fear, guilt, anxiety, lust, greed, pain. It is the old world the prophets have been warning us of, the world that threatens us in our newspapers day by day.

The other world, the new world, is not free of tears; but in the new world, comfort comes from God, and tears are dried. This new world is not free of conflict, but here conflict leads to recon-ciliation rather than revenge. This new world is not free of need, but generosity flows wherever need arises. In short, this new world is the world promised by the prophets. Jesus' secret message tells us, then, that this new world is so possible it is *at hand*, within reach—and as a result, now is the time to rethink everything and begin to learn to live in the ways of the kingdom of God.

This understanding of the secret message of Jesus and its bearing on the future doesn't answer every question or satisfy every wish. It is disappointing as a blueprint of the future. But unlike conventional blueprint understandings, it gives us two things we need—no, three. First, it gives us warning and promise—so that we live life in this world with urgency, awareness, intensity, mission, direction, courage, hope, and vigor. Second, it gives us a sense of empowerment and responsibility, not fatalism and resignation. In other words, it invites us—beginning now—to wake up and live life to the full. Third, it helps us see the kingdom as having come so that we can now enter it, and as still coming so that we diligently and passionately pray for it, welcome it, receive it, and seek it.

And if we seek God's kingdom first and foremost, Jesus promises, we have nothing to worry about.

CHAPTER 20

THE HARVEST OF THE KINGDOM

*The righteous will shine like the sun in
the kingdom of their Father.*
—MATTHEW 13:43

We've said it again and again in these pages: the secret message of Jesus isn't primarily about "heaven after you die." It doesn't give us an exit ramp or escape hatch from this world; rather, it thrusts us back into the here and now so we can be part of God's dreams for planet Earth coming true. But even so, since mortality rates are still pretty high, it's natural for us to ask what the message of the kingdom of God has to say about "heaven after you die."

To answer that question, we need to realize that the word *heaven* works in a number of ways in religious discourse today.[1] First, *heaven* can refer to a place where God is experienced as "present" in a special way.[2] Of course, virtually everyone agrees that God is present everywhere, yet people frequently use the language of place or location to describe a vivid realization or experience of contact with God. They speak of being "in God's presence" as if an omnipresent God had a particular home or headquarters. Even though they know God is everywhere, they speak about God's presence being localized in a house, a temple, a throne, courts, or even a kingdom—all of which in this way become more or less synonymous with *heaven* because they suggest the state of being consciously near or with God. ("Your will be done on earth as it is in heaven" [Matthew 6:10] resonates with this notion—that heaven is the joyful, peaceful place in which God's presence is already experienced so fully that all who are there gladly do God's will.)

Second, *heaven* can refer to a time as well as a place, a *when* as well as a *where*, specifically a time after this life when the spirits of humans who have physically died live on in God's presence. In this sense, "in heaven" can function as much like the phrase "in the summer" (referring to a time) as it functions like the phrase "in Vermont" (referring to a place). And third, *heaven* for many people refers to a state or condition, a *how* as well as a *where* and *when*. It suggests the condition of being without a body, of being in the condition of a disembodied spirit or soul. When people today ask questions about heaven, they're probably referring to a fusion of all these dimensions of the word: being with God (conceived of as a place) after this biological life on planet Earth is over (conceived of as a time) in a disembodied condition (suggested by words like *soul* and *spirit*).[3]

But for Jesus and for most of his contemporaries, the ultimate hope beyond death was not to live forever in a timeless *disembodied* state away from the earth. Instead, they anticipated resurrection, an embodied state within this creation in a new era or age when present wrongs would be made right. If ancient Jews would have thought of a distant, timeless, disembodied state at all, perhaps they would have imagined an intermediate state between death and resurrection, a kind of waiting room where one temporarily stays without a body until the resurrection occurs and one is embodied once again.[4]

The difference between heaven and resurrection may seem trivial to many of us (though it has quite significant ramifications for those who think deeply about it). What concerns many of us is what we will experience, personally, after our pulses and brain waves cease. Does Jesus' message say much about that? The answer depends on what we are looking for. I think many of us are looking for something more akin to detailed reports of "near-death experiences," where we are told exactly what to expect, like a description from someone who just underwent a surgery we need to have soon. We want to hear something like this: "You will breathe your last breath, and then you will feel weightless. Your soul will float out of your body and enter a long, dark tunnel, from which it will emerge into a blinding light. Your entire life will flash before you in an instant. It will be scary at first, but then you will hear a soothing sound . . ."

This desire for specifics is certainly natural, and there is quite a market for it. The unknown frightens us. We want and need comfort and reassurance and hope, especially when facing death. And that is exactly what Jesus offers—and more. Yes, his message is slim on specific details of the postmortem experience, but I'm convinced it yields something even better than what we were looking for—and characteristically, it comes to us hidden in metaphorical language.

One of the most common and evocative metaphors used by Jesus drew from the agrarian experience of Jesus' contemporaries—the annual harvest. Along with increasing numbers of biblical scholars, I've become convinced that Jesus did *not* use the harvest metaphor primarily to describe life after death or the end of the world. Instead, Jesus used harvest language to focus on a close-at-hand, political, historical, and social cataclysm, not a distant, cosmic, end-of-the-world apocalypse. As we saw in chapter 19, the cataclysm Jesus warned them about occurred in AD 67–70, when Zealots launched a violent revolution and the Romans crushed it with brutal force. Life as they knew it was over for the Jewish people, life centered in Jerusalem, temple, priesthood, and homeland. The "end of the age" had come. But when a plant is cut down or harvested and drops its seeds to the ground, those seeds become the hope of a new beginning. That simultaneous ending and new beginning comprise, I think, the primary meaning of harvest language for Jesus.

Even so, I believe the metaphor has a worthwhile secondary application to the question of life after death and the question of the ultimate end of our universe. In this light, life in our world is like a growing season, and eventually harvesttime will come. On a personal level, the good fruit and the ripe grain grown across the seasons of our lives will be harvested and celebrated, and the bad fruit and chaff we've produced will be assessed and discarded as worthless. Many who are seen now as the last and the least— poor, unimportant, unsuccessful—will prove in the end to be first in fruitfulness. Many who appear now to be prosperous, righteous, and successful will then be shown as frauds or pretenders: all leaves and blossoms, but little real fruit.

In this way, the language of harvest evokes the language of final judgment, and final judgment is a highly complex and controversial subject.[5] The image of an ultimate harvest reinforces again and again the idea that there will be a time of accountability (a judgment day) for each of us human beings, but not just for us as individuals. Shockingly to our ears, the image of harvest suggests that God will assess us *as groups as well as individually.*

When Jesus speaks, in Matthew 25 for example, of judging all "the nations" (referring, no doubt, to the Gentile nations), our modern Western mind-set struggles. We tend to see all justice as individual justice. When individuals are required to share responsibility for wrongs committed by the groups to which they belong—wrongs that they didn't personally initiate or perpetrate—we tend to call that unjust.[6] Our Western, individualist preoccupation is unusual in human history, a peculiarity of our current times, politics, psychology, and economics. But in the teachings of Jesus, we must take seriously both individuals and groups, because both individuals and groups are real and must be assessed in the ultimate harvest to determine what is worthy of being preserved and what must be rejected as worthless.

To understand Jesus' distinctive conception of death, the afterlife, and the ultimate harvest, I have found it helpful to contrast his view with those of his contemporaries. We could place Jesus in the center of a diamond (or thinking three-dimensionally, at the apex of a pyramid), seeing his view of the afterlife being at once as similar to and yet radically different from the four alternative positions of his day.

First, the Sadducees believed there was no afterlife. For them, we die and there is nothing beyond death. They loved to ask rhetorical questions that made any kind of afterlife seem implausible. This view engendered a kind of conservatism: *play it safe and take no big risks, because this life is all you've got.* This stance led the Sadducees to cherish their fragile status and prosperity, which led them to protect the status quo and their privileged position in it.

Second, the Pharisees believed there would someday be a resurrection in which the righteous would rise from their graves to enjoy the world-made-new under God's Messiah. Unfortunately, this world-made-new was being kept at bay by the sinfulness of their contemporaries—especially drunks, prostitutes, gluttons, and the like—so the Pharisees cherished their elite spiritual status and treated "sinners" with shame, exclusion, and contempt.

Third, the Hellenists had integrated into their Judaism concepts from the great Greek philosophers (Socrates, Plato,
Aristotle, and others). As a result, they believed that after death,
the immortal souls or spirits of the just would be united with
God in a kind of transcendent, spiritual, disembodied existence.
This led them not to fear death but to see it as an escape from
the suffering of this world. Resurrection—a return to embodied
existence—would be a step down from that transcendent plane,
so it had no place in their thinking. (Many Christians and some
Jews today seem to hold a view similar to this one.)

Fourth, the Zealots believed that the world-made-new could
come only if their countrymen would arise and forcefully seize
power. Those who had the courage to kill and die for the cause
would be resurrected to live again on the earth, enjoying victory
over their enemies.[7] (Their view of the afterlife resonates with
the view of Islamic terrorists today: one gains courage to engage
in violence because one believes violent deeds done for their
religious cause will be rewarded postmortem.)

How does Jesus' view of the afterlife relate to these contemporary options? Like the Zealots, he is willing to sacrifice and die
for his cause because he is confident of resurrection. But unlike
them, he will not inflict violence, and he calls people to love
their enemies, not kill them. Like the Pharisees, Jesus is confident of resurrection, but he envisions a resurrection in which the
outcasts and "sinners" are welcome. This vision of the future
motivates him to befriend and love outcasts and "sinners" in the
present—not isolate himself from and shame them. Like the
Sadducees, Jesus believes we should deal with today's political
and economic realities, but his message never approaches accommodation or complacency, because he believes that death is not
the end. Like the Hellenists, he does not fear death, not because
he envisions an eternity as a disembodied soul, but rather because

he envisions God's harvest as resurrection. His view doesn't make him denigrate creation and anticipate escaping it; instead, it motivates him to give his life to save and heal creation, seeing it as God's treasured work of art.

A central element, then, of Jesus' message—and of his life— is this radical confidence that death is not the end, that this life is not all there is, and that there will be a real resurrection. Paul—building on Jesus' resurrection message—shared this confidence and in one of his letters described it in some detail, echoing Jesus in his use both of the harvest metaphor and of the language of the kingdom of God:

> Christ has indeed been raised from the dead, the firstfruits of those who have fallen asleep. For since death came through a man, the resurrection of the dead comes also through a man. For as in Adam all die, so in Christ all will be made alive. But each in his own turn: Christ, the firstfruits; then, when he comes, those who belong to him. Then the end will come, when he hands over the kingdom to God the Father after he has destroyed all dominion, authority and power. For he must reign until he has put all his enemies under his feet. The last enemy to be destroyed is death. . . . When he has done this, then the Son himself will be made subject to him who put everything under him, so that God may be all in all.
> (1 Corinthians 15:20–26, 28)

For Paul, then, Christ's resurrection was the firstfruits—the first stage of the harvest of all human lives. Jesus' resurrection guarantees that those who belong to him will be raised "when he comes." At that point, he says, the end will come—not "end" in the sense that nothing happens after that point, but rather "end" in the sense of the goal toward which everything is currently

moving. Christ will then hand over the kingdom to God the
Father—after Christ has "destroyed all dominion, authority and
power"—a fascinating phrase that evokes the same language of
"principalities and powers" we explored in chapter 8.

Although a full exploration of this mysterious passage goes
beyond our scope here, it's worth noting how shocking it is to
imagine "all dominion, authority and power" being destroyed—
and portrayed, along with death, as Christ's enemies.[8] Walter
Wink takes seriously this vision of the destruction of "all dominion, authority and power":

> In his Beatitudes, in his extraordinary concern for the outcasts
> and marginalized, in his wholly unconventional treatment of
> women, in his love of children, in his rejection of the belief that
> high-ranking men are the favorites of God, in his subversive
> proclamation of a new order in which domination will give way
> to compassion and communion, Jesus brought to fruition the
> prophetic longing for the "kingdom of God"—an expression we
> might paraphrase as "God's domination-free order."[9]

So here we get an insight into God's ultimate dream: not the
destruction and replacement of this creation, but the destruction
of dominating powers that ruin creation. Freed from these powers,
creation rises again in a "domination-free order." In resonant words
from C. S. Lewis (who thought long and hard on this subject), we
have a picture "not of unmaking but of making. The old field of
space, time, matter, and the senses is to be weeded, dug, and sown
for a new crop. We may be tired of that old field: God is not."[10]

At this point, I must confess that I have a problem: I hear
what Jesus says about afterlife as resurrection—a transformed,
continuing, embodied life in God's creation-made-new—but I
can't begin to imagine *how* it could happen. As soon as I think of

resurrection, a thousand practical questions come to mind (questions similar in many ways to those asked by the Sadducees), including the embarrassingly naive question of where we'd put so many resurrected people from across time!

Paul seems to anticipate these practical questions in 1 Corinthians 15: "How are the dead raised?" he asks (v. 35). But in his answer, he quickly abandons clear prose description and resorts again to harvest metaphor. This "flesh and blood" earthly body, he says, is planted in death like a seed in soil. The "heavenly body" that grows from the seed is as unlike (yet as related to) our current body as a stalk of wheat is unlike (yet as related to) the seed from which it germinated. There is continuity, but also discontinuity. What is perishable, dishonorable, and weak is raised imperishable, glorious, and powerful. Paul tries to explain further, but finally he seems to give up rational analysis and resorts to an ecstatic outburst of praise (a habit I also notice elsewhere in his writings): "'Death has been swallowed up in victory.' 'Where, O death, is your victory? Where, O death, is your sting?' . . . But thanks be to God! He gives us the victory through our Lord Jesus Christ" (vv. 54–55, 57).

So both Jesus and Paul's excursions into what the resurrection will be like fail to satisfy my curiosity for detail—as, no doubt, this chapter will fail to satisfy yours. But that's okay. Perhaps we don't need to be able to fully picture it. Perhaps details would preoccupy us, distract us from where our focus should be. Perhaps all we need is the challenge, the invitation, the enticement to risk everything in faith for this vision of an eternal creative project of God . . . to see the only reward worth having as the reward of being part of the kingdom of God, both now in this life and after death too.

I must also confess my uneasiness with that word *reward* in the previous sentence. As C. S. Lewis said (using *heaven* to include resurrection), "We are afraid that heaven is a bribe," and we fear that talk of rewards will make us selfish, mercenary, and small. But, Lewis says:

> It is not so. Heaven offers nothing that a mercenary soul can desire. It is safe to tell the pure in heart that they shall see God, for only the pure in heart want to. There are rewards that do not sully motives. A man's love for a woman is not mercenary because he wants to marry her, nor his love for poetry mercenary because he wants to read it, nor his love of exercise less disinterested because he wants to run and leap and walk. Love, by definition, seeks to enjoy its object.[11]

Jesus often promises that his followers will enjoy great rewards—rewards for being persecuted, for loving enemies, for giving to the poor and praying and fasting in secret, for welcoming a prophet, for giving a cup of cold water to a disciple, for making sacrifices of family and property and security for him. In one extravagant case, he says, "I tell you the truth, at the renewal of all things, when the Son of Man sits on his glorious throne, . . . everyone who has left houses or brothers or sisters or father or mother or wife or children or fields for my sake will receive a hundred times as much and will inherit eternal life" (Matthew 19:28–29). On this subject of rewards, Lewis further muses:

> Indeed, if we consider the unblushing promises of reward and the staggering nature of the rewards promised in the Gospels, it would seem that our Lord finds our desire, not too strong, but too weak. We are half-hearted creatures, fooling about with drink and sex and ambition when infinite joy is offered us, like an ignorant child who wants to go on making mud pies in a slum because he cannot imagine what is meant by the offer of

a holiday at the sea. We are far too easily pleased. . . . There are different kinds of rewards. . . . The proper rewards are not simply tacked on to the activity for which they are given, but are the activity itself in consummation.[12]

So the ultimate hope beyond death is the hope of resurrection, which is the hope of consummation, the hope of sharing in "the renewal of all things." All we have been desiring all our lives, all we have been reaching for, working for, sacrificing for, and suffering for in our pursuit of the kingdom of God, will finally and fully come to us. Our dreams, hopes, labors, and love will be consummated, fulfilled, and rewarded in the kingdom of God in this broadest sense, which comprises this life and what we call the afterlife in one awesome reality.

With that understanding, I finally find myself able to turn from speculating about details. I instead find myself increasingly motivated—*magnetized* is a better word—to seek, fit in with, and live God's plans and mission in this life. And interestingly, this is exactly the practical conclusion Paul draws in the passage we've been exploring: "Therefore, my dear brothers, stand firm. Let nothing move you. Always give yourselves fully to the work of the Lord, because you know that your labor in the Lord is not in vain" (1 Corinthians 15:58).

We shouldn't be surprised that our curiosity about "the end" (the ultimate goal) of all things—and of our individual lives—always turns our attention from esoteric speculation back to practical daily life. Our vision of the ultimate harvest sets our hearts on seeking God's kingdom first and foremost here and now, giving ourselves fully to "the work of the Lord," to our "labor in the Lord"—since not one grain of the harvest will be wasted, nor one shred of effort or sacrifice be "in vain." That pattern—looking ahead to the ultimate harvest, but then coming back to life and fruitfulness in the here and now—again seems to be at the heart of Jesus' secret message, as we've seen chapter after chapter.[13]

Some scientists tell us that our universe faces one of two unhappy endings: a big freeze or a big, hot crunch. Either way, many scientists predict that long before the big freeze or big crunch, our planet and all life on it will be incinerated when our sun goes supernova. And long before that, each of us will die. With these gloomy scenarios in mind, you can't help but remember the words of the great philosopher Woody Allen: "Today we are at a crossroads. One road leads to hopelessness and despair; the other, to total extinction. Let us pray we choose wisely." Happily, the secret message of Jesus offers us an additional glorious option: that we are invited to participate with God and others in the creation of a glorious harvest of joy, peace, justice, and love, in a glorious story that never, ever ends.[14]

The adjective used three times in the previous sentence—*glorious*—provides the best ending point for this exploration of what Jesus' message says about life after death. The word evokes two physical realities: weight and luminosity. This weight and luminosity help explain why biblical passages that speak of the ultimate harvest of the kingdom so often include extravagant imagery, such as gold and precious stones, substances that combine weight with shimmer and glow. C. S. Lewis explains:

> All the scriptural imagery (harps, crowns, gold, etc.) is, of course, a merely symbolical attempt to express the inexpressible. Musical instruments are mentioned because for many people (not all) music is the thing known in this present life which most strongly suggests ecstasy and infinity. Crowns are mentioned to suggest the fact that those who are united with God in eternity share His splendor and power and joy. Gold is

mentioned to suggest the timelessness of Heaven (gold does not rust) and the preciousness of it. People who take these symbols literally might as well think that when Christ told us to be like doves, He meant that we were to lay eggs.[15]

But what is the essence of this glory? Again, Lewis says it so well: the essence of glory is to be a source of delight for God, a harvest God takes pride in, a part of God's dream coming true. I can't grasp this with my little brain. In fact, I can barely begin to imagine it, but I feel that one of the most important things I can do is to try, to reach, to dream. As Lewis says:

I read in a periodical the other day that the fundamental thing is how we think of God. By God Himself, it is not! How God thinks of us is not only more important, but infinitely more important. Indeed how we think of Him is of no importance except insofar as it is related to how He thinks of us. It is written that we shall "stand before" Him, shall appear, shall be inspected. The promise of glory is the promise, almost incredible and only possible by the work of Christ, that some of us, that any of us who really chooses, shall actually survive that examination, shall find approval, shall please God. To please God . . . to be a real ingredient in the divine happiness . . . to be loved by God, not merely pitied, but delighted in as an artist delights in his work or a father in a son—it seems impossible, a weight or burden of glory which our thoughts can hardly sustain. But so it is.[16]

CHAPTER 21

SEEING THE KINGDOM

To you has been given the secret of the kingdom of God.
—Mark 4:11 ESV

It's early summer as I write these words that will be part of the last chapter of this book. (I have a lot of editing to do before the book is complete though!) We've had some beautiful weather here in Maryland in recent weeks—perfect weather for sleeping with the windows open. About 4:30 or so each June morning, just before dawn, I often am awakened to the sound of birds singing. My neighborhood is gloriously full of birds. I'm not annoyed when they awaken me; I consider it a gift. I love to lie there and listen, picking out familiar voices: robins—lots of them, mockingbirds—lots of them too, and plenty of English sparrows. Then, if I keep listening, I hear more . . . a Carolina wren, a house wren (one of my favorites), a house finch, a song sparrow, then of course a few crows, maybe a grackle, some mourning doves, and if I'm very fortunate, from the forest at the end of my street I might hear the distant call of a wood thrush. Earlier in the season, I heard the unmistakable sounds of a flock of cedar waxwings passing through on their way north. I never saw them, but by the high chatter of their unique song, I knew they had passed by as I lay in bed.

Before I learned the distinctive call of these common birds, I heard the sound, but I didn't know what I was hearing. The notes all mixed together. It was as impossible then to unthread one song from another as it is now for me *not* to distinguish their unique songs. Once you learn the call of a bluebird or a bobolink or a red-winged blackbird or an indigo bunting or a rufous-sided towhee, you can't *not* identify it.

I wonder if the secret message of Jesus isn't like that. Maybe you've been hearing it all along, but you didn't realize it. Maybe you've been seeing it or seeing signs of it, but you didn't know what you were seeing. Maybe the best outcome of this book is that your ears and eyes—your heart and mind—will have been in some way "born again," so that you will now and forever know it when you hear it or see it, when it comes near and sings its song in the high branches.

If the great religious writer Huston Smith is right, there is something in us that is incapable of being satisfied until we get to the meaning of a certain secret, what he calls "the longing":

> There is within us—in even the blithest, most lighthearted among us—a fundamental dis-ease. . . . This desire lies in the marrow of our bones and deep in the regions of our soul. All great literature, poetry, art, philosophy, psychology, and religion tries to name and analyze this longing. We are seldom in direct touch with it, and indeed the modern world seems set on preventing us from getting in touch with it by covering it with . . . entertainments, obsessions, and distractions of every sort. But the longing is there, built into us like a jack-in-the-box

that presses for release. . . . Whether we realize it or not, simply to be human is to long for release from mundane existence with its confining walls of finitude and mortality. The Good News . . . is that that longing can be fulfilled.[1]

What is that unnamed longing for? A thousand things, yet one thing. C. S. Lewis simply described it as *beauty*:

We do not want merely to see beauty, though, God knows, even that is bounty enough. We want something else which can hardly be put into words—to be united with the beauty we see, to pass into it, to receive it into ourselves, to bathe in it, to become part of it. . . . At present we are on the outside of the world, the wrong side of the door. We discern the freshness and purity of morning, but they do not make us fresh and pure. We cannot mingle with the splendors we see. But all the leaves of the New Testament are rustling with the rumor that it will not always be so. Some day, God willing, we shall get *in*.[2]

It is my conviction, after these many years of reflecting on the secret message of Jesus, that what Smith, Lewis, and a thousand other writers, poets, teachers, and mystics have been talking about is hidden like a treasure in this beautiful phrase, "kingdom of God." It surprises us at unexpected moments, sings like a bird, sparkles like light on water—real, there, yet only a glimmer.

The glimpses are brief, momentary. We wish they would stay so we could capture them and keep them, but by their very elusiveness, they instead capture us. Emily Dickinson perhaps understood why it must be this way: "Like lightning to the children eased / Through revelation kind, / The truth must dazzle gradually / Or every man be blind." Like the scent of the ocean when you are still miles away, or the hint of springtime you catch on a mild day when winter is still here, or like a childhood memory that you didn't even know was still there until in the kitchen one day you smell the mixture of coffee percolating and bread baking and it all comes back . . . a glimpse or scent or song of the kingdom will "dazzle gradually." As my friend Samir Selmanovic says, "These glimpses put a splinter in our heart, and once we get a glimpse of the kingdom of God, nothing else will ever fully satisfy us." We are incurably afflicted with the desire to see more, and more, and more. We are converted into seekers of God's kingdom.

These glimpses of the kingdom of God come to us unpredictably, unexpectedly—maybe in a book or even a sermon. For me recently, one such glimpse came as I read the word "jail" in this passage from one of Frederick Buechner's sermons:

> The Kingdom of God? Time after time Jesus tries to drum into our heads what he means by it. He heaps parable upon parable like a madman. He tries shouting it. He tries whispering it. . . . What he seems to be saying is that the Kingdom of God is the time, or a time beyond time, when it will no longer be humans in their lunacy who are in charge of the world but God in his mercy who will be in charge of the world. It's the time above all else for wild rejoicing—like getting out of jail, like being cured of cancer, like finally, at long last, coming home. And it is at hand, Jesus says.[3]

I think that the best glimpses of the kingdom of God come to us unexpectedly in everyday life—and the sermons we hear (or books we read) help us keep our eyes open so that when those moments come, we don't sleepwalk through them. Buechner himself describes one such experience—in Orlando, Florida, of all places, at a tourist attraction called Sea World:

It was a gorgeous day when we were there, with bright Florida sunlight reflected in the shimmering water and a cloudless blue sky over our heads. The bleachers where we sat were packed. The way the show began was that at a given signal they released into the tank five or six killer whales, as we call them (it would be interesting to know what they call us), and no creatures under heaven could have looked less killer-like as they went racing around and around in circles. What with the dazzle of sky and sun, the beautiful young people on the platform, the soft southern air, and the crowds all around us watching the performance with a delight matched only by what seemed the delight of the performing whales, it was as if the whole creation—men and women and beasts and sun and water and earth and sky and, for all I know, God himself—was caught up in one great, jubilant dance of unimaginable beauty. And then, right in the midst of it, I was astonished to find that my eyes were filled with tears.[4]

Buechner then turned to his wife and daughter and told them of this rush of emotion, and they replied that they felt the same thing. What was it that day on the bleachers of Sea World that touched them, teared them up? He explains:

We shed tears because we had caught a glimpse of the Peaceable Kingdom, and it had almost broken our hearts. For a few minutes we had seen Eden and been a part of the great dance that goes on at the heart of creation. We shed tears because we were given a glimpse of the way life was created to be and is not. . . . Joy is home, and I believe the tears that came to our eyes were more than anything else homesick tears.[5]

On another occasion, it was in another unlikely place, as different from Sea World as one could imagine. It was in heavy traffic, driving into New York City, when Buechner felt he had a glimpse of the kingdom:

> For a moment it was not the world as it is that I saw but the world as it might be, as something deep within the world wants to be and is preparing to be, the way in darkness a seed prepares for growth, the way leaven works in bread.[6]

These moments of seeing—these glimpses of insight into the kingdom—can't be conjured or created. They can only be received. And similarly, the kingdom itself—what "the world wants to be and is preparing to be"—can't be achieved, but only received:

> Humanly speaking, if we have any chance to survive, I suspect that it is men and women who act out of that deep impulse [which is best described with words like *tolerance, compassion, sanity, hope, justice*] who are our chance. By no means will they themselves bring about the Kingdom of God. It is God alone who brings about his Kingdom. . . . We cannot make the Kingdom of God happen, but we can put out leaves as it draws near. We can be kind to each other. We can be kind to ourselves. We can drive back the darkness a little. We can make green places within ourselves and among ourselves where God can make his Kingdom happen.[7]

There is a moment when I often feel the rush of the grandeur of the kingdom of God. It comes not through my eyes but through my ears, in Handel's *Messiah* during the "Hallelujah Chorus." This moment is not, for me, when the voices sing out, fortissimo and glorious, "Hallelujah! Hallelujah!" again and again, as wonderful as that is. Nor is it that beautiful section when the melody seems to ascend triumphantly over the words "For the Lord

God omnipotent reigneth"—although that is splendid indeed. My moment comes just after this loud, glorious, powerful, moving section. The tone shifts and these words are sung—softly, gently, slowly, and smoothly—in a gradual swell, growing in intensity, descending and ascending in tone like so many waves in a rising tide, culminating in a momentous finality: "The kingdom of this world is become the kingdom of our Lord, and of his Christ, and of his Christ, and he shall reign forever and ever."

These words from Revelation 11:15 evoke an understanding of the kingdom of God very different from the one many people seem to have, if they have any understanding at all. For them, the words should actually go, "The kingdom of this world is destroyed, and in its place the kingdom of God goes on in heaven." In contrast, the glimpse we're given in this moment is not of the end of the space-time universe but rather of its transformation, not its destruction but its salvation, not its replacement but its fulfillment.[8]

I'm not completely sure why this line so grabs my heart. Perhaps it's the idea that nothing will be wasted, that this universe—so precious, so wonderful, so amazing—won't be discarded and destroyed like an old paper cup, whether in a big, deep freeze or a singular, hot crunch. Rather, it will be saved from decay, saved from corruption, saved from evil, and transformed. These words make me happy for "the kingdom of this world" because it will someday be liberated from all domination and will become what it has always wanted to be, always groaned to be, always dreamed of being.

And more . . . these words even make me, on some deep level, happy for Jesus. He tried and tried to tell us in word and deed, in sign and wonder, in metaphor and parable, but we were so dull. But if Revelation is right, our dullness will not prevail.

And more still . . . these words make me happy for God. Like a mother dreaming a good future for the baby at her breast, like a father standing at the crib watching his newborn sleep peacefully, God will see God's own primal dream for creation finally coming true—and that dream won't be imposed by God from outside by domination against creation's will, but it will emerge from within creation itself, so that God's dream and creation's groaning for fulfillment are one. God's creation will finally be—as a whole and in all its parts—good, beautiful, and true. It will be harmonious and diverse, dynamic and healthy, generative and fruitful, novel and wonderful. Its evil will be judged and purged, its harvest will be celebrated. And of course, these words fail.

Perhaps all along, my deepest joy has never been to have all my dreams come true, but rather to have God's one dream come true: *that this world will become a place God is at home in, a place God takes pride and pleasure in, a place where God's dreams come true.*

But no, that's not exactly what the text says. It puts it not in the future tense but in the present perfect: *The kingdom of this world is (or has) become the kingdom of our Lord and of his Messiah.* We look around us, and what do we see? Not the present, perfect. Not the kingdom of God, fully come. Instead, we see regimes of violence, threat, abuse, conflict, danger, pollution, corruption, domination, and oppression. The kingdom has not yet fully come. There is much to do—beginning with our realizing that there is such a thing, such a possibility, as the kingdom of God, and adjusting and arranging our lives to be part of it, to seek it, to work with it and for it.

So often we do not see it. But then, suddenly, we do. We look with our hearts, not just our eyes, and there it is, as if it had been there all along, among us, within us, near, here: the kingdom of this world *has become* the kingdom of our Lord and of his Christ, his Messiah, his liberating King. The world has not yet become the kingdom, and yet *we see that it has.*

It is in that tension—perhaps the most truly creative tension in the world—that the secret message of Jesus dances, glimmers, shines, and calls us to live: seeing the kingdom here, and seeking and praying for it to come. As we pray for it to come, we might consider using as a model for our prayers the simple but profound prayer that Jesus first taught his disciples. This prayer, found in Matthew 6, has become almost invisible to many of us because it is so familiar; it is memorized and recited so often that many people have never asked themselves what it means. In light of all we've considered together in these pages, perhaps we can see it (again) for the first time.

I recommend we savor each phrase of this prayer, allowing it to capture and inspire our imagination and transform our aspirations, giving us a vision of the kingdom. If enough of us see the kingdom—and seeing it, rethink our lives, and rethinking our lives, believe that the impossible is possible—everything could change.

> Our Father in heaven,
> hallowed be your name,
> your kingdom come,
> your will be done on earth as it is in heaven.
> Give us today our daily bread.
> Forgive us our debts, as we also have forgiven our debtors.
> And lead us not into temptation, but deliver us from the
>   evil one.

AFTERWORD

I must preach the good news of the kingdom of God . . .
for I was sent for this purpose.
—LUKE 4:43 ESV

There is so much more to say about the secret message of Jesus. It has far-reaching implications for the widest range of subjects—from racism to ecology, from weapons proliferation to terrorism, from interreligious conflict to destructive entertainment, from education to economics, from sexuality to art, from politics to technology, from liturgy to contemplation. We have only scratched the surface here.

I take some comfort in the poem "A Future Not Our Own" by Archbishop Oscar Romero of El Salvador, who was assassinated for speaking up for God's kingdom and justice in 1980:

> It helps, now and then, to step back
> and take the long view.
> The kingdom is not only beyond our efforts,
> it is beyond our vision.

We accomplish in our lifetime only a tiny fraction of
the magnificent enterprise that is God's work.
Nothing we do is complete,
which is another way of saying
that the kingdom always lies beyond us.

No statement says all that could be said.
No prayer fully expresses our faith.
No confession brings perfection . . .
No set of goals and objectives includes everything.

This is what we are about:
We plant seeds that one day will grow.
We water seeds already planted,
knowing that they hold future promise.
We lay foundations that will need further development.
We provide yeast that produces effects beyond our capabilities.

We cannot do everything
and there is a sense of liberation in realizing that.
This enables us to do something,
and to do it very well.
It may be incomplete, but it is a beginning, a step along the way,
an opportunity for God's grace to enter and do the rest.

We may never see the end results . . .
We are prophets of a future not our own.

This book is my "something . . . It may be incomplete, but
it is a beginning." I think of Jesus in his parables. He seems
more interested in stirring curiosity than in completely satisfying it—in making people hungry and thirsty for more rather

than making them feel complacently stuffed. Perhaps that's how it should be.

Whatever we learn about the secret message of Jesus should make us want to seek more, learn more, experience more—and not just to understand it from a book, but to "get into it" by living it. I suppose it's like golf or fishing or playing the violin or being married or raising children or skydiving or falling in love or being alive: you can read books about it, but that's not the real point. Don't you think?

WHY DIDN'T WE GET IT SOONER?

There will be weeping there, and gnashing of teeth, when you see
Abraham, Isaac and Jacob and all the prophets in the kingdom of
God, but you yourselves thrown out. People will come from east and
west and north and south, and will take their places at the feast in
the kingdom of God. Indeed there are those who are last who
will be first, and first who will be last.

—LUKE 13:28–30

This understanding of Jesus' secret message is certainly not original. I'm sure I never would have had the courage to question my conventional interpretations of Jesus' teachings if it weren't for a number of biblical scholars and theologians whose writings tapped into my own suppressed disquiet—the sense that there was more going on in Jesus' life and teachings than my conventional theology could access. In particular, the writings of Dallas Willard, Bishop N. T. Wright, Walter Wink, John Howard Yoder, and Walter Brueggemann stimulated my thinking. But there have been so many others—Sharon Welch, Howard Snyder, Brian Hathaway, Jim Wallis, John Perkins, Tony Campolo, Tim King, Todd Hunter . . . too many to name.[1]

But all of these writers are contemporary, you might notice, which would prompt a legitimate question: if this reading of the Gospels is accurate, why didn't scholars see it a hundred or five hundred or eighteen hundred years ago? Critics might reply that the answer is obvious: this reading isn't rooted in the text of the Gospels at all; it's like a smudge on the glasses of recent scholars, saying more about our contemporary perspective than about Jesus himself. It's not something read from the text, critics might judge, but rather something read into the text. This judgment is certainly possible. After all, people have read all kinds of things into Jesus' teachings—from reincarnation to white supremacy to Americanism to how to get rich quick to who knows what.

I don't believe this criticism is legitimate—for two reasons. First, we have to ask what makes a good reading good. It's hard to try to answer such an important and profound question in a sentence, but let me offer one sentence that says much in spite of its brevity. *A good reading accounts for more of the details included in the text than a bad reading.*[2] This reading of the biblical text—that at the heart of Jesus' message is this rich and radical idea of the kingdom of God being "at hand" and "coming down" here and now—accounts for far more of the biblical text than any other I've seen. Traditional readings, which assume Jesus has come primarily to solve the timeless problem of original sin so we can go "up" to a timeless heaven "by and by" after we die, do indeed account for some of Jesus' words and actions, but not with the intensity and resonance of this reading.

Second, other contemporary readings—some of them quite en vogue these days—seem to reduce the text to those passages that fit with one "angle" or another, creating images of Jesus that are either mirror images of the scholars who propose them or a rather two-dimensional character who is easy to dismiss. In contrast, our reading here takes the whole text in all its wildness and intensity and seems to integrate political, social, theological, eschatological, and other themes into one coherent whole. In my opinion, it brings the text together and makes sense of its details as no other reading I've ever come across.

The question still remains: why hasn't this reading arisen sooner? There are reasons to believe that this kind of reading simply *could not have arisen* previously. Those reasons do not include any arrogant or naive notions that we in the twenty-first century are somehow better or smarter or more enlightened than our sisters and brothers from times past. Standing on their shoulders, then, we look back and consider a number of possible reasons for our slowness to see the message of the kingdom. In fact, without their legacy we couldn't see what we now see.

First, early in church history (by the end of the second century, for sure), the Christian faith took a fateful turn. It went from being a Jewish sect, committed to maintaining complete continuity with historic Judaism, to becoming a Gentile religion with persistent anti-Semitic tendencies. It pains me to say this, but any church historian must admit this is the case. That anti-Semitism tended to blind Christians from the uniquely Jewish dimensions of the story of Jesus and of his teaching—the very dimensions that have enriched our story. Perhaps then, the anti-Semitism all too common in church history prohibited readers from understanding Jesus' secret message because it is a radically Jewish message. Anti-Semitism would also lead to disinterest in and ignorance of the first-century setting in which Jesus lived and taught. That ignorance would make this kind of reading unlikely if not impossible. (It may be too much to hope that this reappraisal of Jesus and his message by Christians like myself could make possible new common ground for Jewish-Christian dialogue. Realistic or not, this is my hope.)

Second, the church's early divorce from Jewish roots was

accompanied by a corresponding love affair with Greek philosophy. Greek philosophy—especially in the Neoplatonic stream in which many early Christian thinkers were immersed—was more interested in universal concepts than particulars, more focused on timeless truths than timely ones. This mind-set would predispose readers of the Gospels to interpret Jesus' message as a set of timeless abstractions and miss the historically particular references to contemporary political realities and social movements.[3]

Contrast the flood of man-hours spent by the church debating esoteric theological/philosophical issues with the comparative trickle of attention paid to understanding and applying Jesus' kingdom ethics; the difference is staggering—and in light of our exploration here, heartbreaking. Some might argue that the esoteric arguments were necessary; otherwise, Christian theology would have lost its doctrinal integrity and become a subset of some other ideology. But if it did indeed succeed in saving its doctrinal integrity, one wonders if it lost its ethical integrity in the process, and one wonders what profit there is in saving the former while losing the latter.

Third, in the early fourth century, Christianity was embraced by the emperor Constantine (whether sincerely or manipulatively for political expediency, we can only speculate). After its divorce from Judaism and affair with Neoplatonic philosophy, Christianity now entered a lasting marriage with Constantine's empire. Now as the official religion of the Roman Empire, how could it read the teachings of Jesus as being critical of the empire? No wonder the scholars of the church would drift into "safer" abstract readings that didn't question the status quo—since they now were so thoroughly affiliated with and deeply wedded to the very "principalities and powers" that Jesus and his apostles said the kingdom of God had come to overturn.

No doubt there were certain advantages—and perhaps even

inevitabilities—to this liaison of church and empire. Taking into account all of the historical dynamics, it's hard to imagine other better story lines any of us could have created without un-intended negative consequences of their own; it's hard to imagine what we could have done differently, even knowing what we know. But the fact remains that much was lost through this unhappy marriage. Walter Wink puts it poignantly:

> What Jesus envisioned was a world transformed. . . . If Jesus had never lived, we would not have been able to invent him. The world, and even the church, had no categories for such funda-mental change. It is no wonder that the radicality of Jesus was soon watered down by the church. . . . The church no longer saw the demonic as lodged in the empire, but in the empire's enemies. Because society was now regarded as Christian, atone-ment became a highly individual transaction between the believer and God. The idea that the work of Christ involves the radical critique of society was largely abandoned.[4]

Fourth, as we have seen, with this alliance between church and empire came an endorsement of the use of violence in the service of the kingdom of God. It's hard to imagine getting anything right about Jesus' secret message when the church/empire concluded that heretics could be justly tortured using many of the most hor-rific methods ever invented—evisceration, stripping of the skin, burning, and the like. Add to this tragedy the repeated incursions of violent "barbarians"—Huns, Goths, Vikings, and so on—along with repeated wars with Muslims, and it's clear that the church was so desperately fighting for survival that it was unlikely to consider alternative understandings of Jesus' teachings even if they were proposed. In fact, it's easy to imagine how alternative understand-ings proposed in wartime would be equated with treason. And since literacy during these dark times was rare, there wouldn't be a surplus of scholars with time on their hands to explore out-of-the-box understandings of the message of Jesus.

Fifth, after the Middle Ages, when Protestants broke with the Western church, most new segments of the church simply created new alliances with the secular state, so that instead of one Holy Roman Empire, we had many church-state liaisons. Christendom in these contexts metamorphosed into various new forms of civil religion, each a willing servant of nationalism. Considering Jesus' words about the impossibility of serving two masters, none of these options would prove compatible with the secret message of Jesus. In these contexts, proclaiming the secret message of Jesus as we have considered it here would not only be judged unorthodox; it would also be condemned as un-patriotic—and therefore largely unthinkable. (Some readers may have felt this very objection as they read this book, because civil religion is still dominant in many quarters.)

A sixth important factor: it wasn't until recent decades that new documents from the ancient world were discovered and trans-lated, including the Dead Sea Scrolls. These documents have given us more and more insight into the religious, political, and social times in which Jesus lived. Without those documents and the scholarship surrounding them, it was too easy to assume that conventional understandings had taken everything into account and left no room for rethinking. Meanwhile, there have been several intensifications of the "quest for the historical Jesus" in recent centuries. Again, these quests too often created a Jesus cast more or less in the image of those doing the scholarship: a ratio-nalist Jesus, a romantic Jesus, and so on. It takes time for bad or biased scholarship to be sorted out from good and for the slices of good scholarship to be in some way integrated with one another—and most importantly, with the biblical text itself. This process is ongoing and suggests that the vision of Jesus' message we've considered here will need continuing development in the years to come.

Seventh, until recent decades, the Christian church may not have acknowledged enough mistakes to do any serious self-examination. (No doubt it had made plenty of mistakes, but it had not acknowledged very many.) During the period of colonization, the Western church in both its Protestant and Catholic forms was energized by an expanding sense of mission (mission too often hybridized, sadly, with colonization itself). Like a team in the middle of a winning season or a rock band ascending to superstardom, a religion expanding in partnership with colonization does not find itself in a highly reflective mode, especially about the injustices associated with colonization itself.[5]

But when failures mount and when some failures rise to the level of scandals and atrocities (the conquest and genocide of Native Americans, the global slave trade, American slavery and segregation, South African apartheid, environmental degradation, two world wars, the Holocaust, the death toll of Japanese noncombatants when the United States dropped nuclear bombs on Hiroshima and Nagasaki, pedophilia scandals, and so on), organizations tend to become more reflective. Declining numbers can have a similar effect. "What went wrong?" becomes "What's wrong with us?" which in turn can lead to "What's wrong with our message?" Pride goes before a fall, and perhaps proud organizations need a fall before they are open to repentance or rethinking.

There's at least one more reason that must be considered in answer to the question we're considering here: every religion, *including Christianity*, can become an opponent to the secret message of Jesus. A leader in the Bruderhof Communities, Christoph Friedrich Blumhardt (1842–1919), understood this danger: "Nothing is more dangerous to the advancement of God's kingdom than religion. But this is what Christianity has become. Do you not know it is possible to kill Christ with such Christianity?"

The great Danish philosopher Søren Kierkegaard offered a similarly provocative diagnosis:

> The matter is quite simple. The Bible is very easy to under-stand. But we Christians are a bunch of scheming swindlers. We pretend to be unable to understand it because we know very well that the minute we understand we are obliged to act accordingly. Take any words in the New Testament and forget everything except pledging yourself to act accordingly. My God, you will say, if I do that my whole life will be ruined. How would I ever get on in the world?
>
> Herein lies the real place of Christian scholarship. Christian scholarship is the Church's prodigious invention to defend itself against the Bible, to ensure that we can continue to be good Christians without the Bible coming too close. Dreadful it is to fall into the hands of the living God. Yes, it is even dreadful to be alone with the New Testament.[6]

A Christian like myself can't help but read Blumhardt's and Kierkegaard's words with a feeling of bitter shame—and with immense gratitude for the New Testament! As Walter Wink has said, "Nevertheless, the story was there for all to read in the Gospels, and it continues to work, like a time-release capsule."[7]

What was true for Jesus' contemporaries—that they could miss the kingdom while those from "east and west and north and south" would come in and enjoy the feast—could certainly be true for adherents to the Christian religion today. Wouldn't it be fascinating if thousands of Muslims, alienated with where funda-mentalists and extremists have taken their religion, began to "take their places at the feast," discovering the secret message of

Jesus in ways that many Christians have not? Could it be that Jesus, always recognized as one of the greatest prophets of Islam, could in some way be rediscovered to save Islam from its dangerous dark side? Similarly, wouldn't there be a certain ironic justice if Jesus' own kinsmen, the Jewish people, led the way in understanding and practicing the core teaching of one of their own prophets who has too often been hijacked by other interests or ideologies? Or if Buddhists, Hindus, and even former atheists and agnostics came from "east and west and north and south" and began to enjoy the feast of the kingdom in ways that those bearing the name *Christian* have not?[8] Of course, because we have the "time-release capsule" of the New Testament, there is always hope that we Christians will not be the last to rediscover the truth that could change everything. Perhaps the blandly moralistic traditionalism of some of our churches and the angry, fearful, militant arrogance of others have become sufficiently distasteful that we are closer to a rediscovery than we might realize.

Perhaps just as it took us more than eighteen hundred years to have the courage to face what the message of Jesus meant for slavery, and another hundred to begin to ask what it means for women, and another hundred to begin to ask what it means for the environment—perhaps it always takes time for us to be ready to see what has been there all along. One thinks of the famous, passionate words of John Robinson, as he said goodbye to those of his congregation who were setting sail for America on the *Mayflower* in 1620:

I charge you before God . . . that you follow me no further than you have seen me follow the Lord Jesus Christ. If God reveals anything to you by any other instrument of His, be as ready to receive it as you were to receive any truth by my ministry, for I am verily persuaded the Lord hath more truth yet to break forth out of His Holy Word. For my part, I cannot sufficiently bewail the condition of those reformed churches which . . . will go, at present, no further than the instruments of their reformation. The Lutherans cannot be drawn to go beyond what Luther saw; whatever part of His will our God had revealed to Calvin, they will rather die than embrace it; and the Calvinists, you see, stick fast where they were left by that great man of God, who yet saw not all things. This is a misery much to be lamented.

If Robinson's words are still true nearly four centuries later—that Scripture has more treasures than we have yet realized—then the fresh understanding of the kingdom of God we have explored in these pages is surely not the end of an adventure. It's not like we can finally pat one another on the back and say, "Now we see everything, don't we?" Rather, a renewal of interest in the secret message of Jesus could mark the early beginnings of a new chapter in history, the birth of an unspeakably important adventure—an exploration that could change everything.

APPENDIX 2

PLOTTING GOODNESS

The kingdom of heaven is like treasure hidden in a field,
which a man found and covered up. Then in his joy he
goes and sells all that he has and buys that field.
—MATTHEW 13:44 ESV

I hope this book has not satisfied your curiosity about the secret message of Jesus. Instead, I hope it has stoked the flame of your curiosity as never before. I hope, as a result, that you'll want to continue exploring the message and its meaning for your life and for our world. Here are three next steps I'd recommend:

1. *Gather for conversation.* The kingdom of God was originally explored in a group of twelve, and that still seems to be the best way. You don't need twelve, but why not encourage a few friends to read this book and then meet to discuss it together? It might be some friends at work who meet over breakfast or lunch one day a week, or some friends from your church or neighborhood who meet in your dining room or living room. Or maybe you know some people who regularly could gather at a coffee shop or pub for some good dialogue. You could agree on a reading plan—maybe a chapter a week—and then give each person ten

(or however many) minutes to share his or her reactions to the week's chapter: sharing quotes, raising questions or disagreements, or relating ideas in this book to his or her own life.

Or you could agree to underline passages of special interest and take turns sharing underlined passages and why you considered them interesting. Or you could actually read the chapter aloud together and then take turns answering certain queries about each chapter—queries like these:

- What did you like best?
- What didn't you understand?
- What didn't you agree with?
- What seems most relevant to your life?
- What questions does this chapter raise for further study or discussion?

After you've discussed the whole book, you could progress to reading the original four Gospels. I'd recommend you read a chapter aloud together (either taking turns or reading aloud in unison); there is something about the Gospels that comes alive when they're read aloud as a storyteller would tell them.[1] Or you could give everyone a half hour to read the chapter silently, taking notes and writing down responses in preparation for your dialogue. Then you could answer the queries above or try some of these:

- What does this passage tell you about God?
- What does it tell you about the kingdom of God?
- What does it tell you about Jesus?
- What does it tell you about yourself?
- What does it tell you about our mission in the world?
- What questions does this passage raise for further study and discussion?

Many groups find it best to sign on for a time commitment—say, three months or a year. If your group jells and seems to take on a life of its own, enjoy the ride! If new people keep joining the group (which is a good thing, since a good secret like this should be shared), you may need to divide into subgroups (four is a good number for each subgroup) to facilitate conversation. You might start with one group at the kitchen table and soon have foursomes meeting in the living room, dining room, and basement, or you might begin in a corner of a pub or coffee shop and soon expand to several tables.[2]

2. *Launch experiments.* It's not enough just to read, study, and discuss the secret message of Jesus; it is meant to be *practiced.* So, as part of your group conversation, you could agree to launch certain experiments where you agree to try practicing some facet of Jesus' teaching over the next week and then report on your experiences—your successes, failures, surprises, reflections, and conclusions—the next time you gather. For example, you might experiment with the following:

- "Turning the other cheek" for a week: responding to mistreatment with neither retaliation nor retreat but rather with creative exposure and transcendence.
- Praying for and blessing (speaking kindly to) people who mistreat you.
- Using simple, plain speech: not making vows, speaking with sensitive yet unvarnished honesty, letting your 'Yes' be 'Yes' and your 'No,' 'No' (Matthew 5:37).
- Doing to others as you would have them do to you.
- Not judging anyone or calling anyone stupid or foolish.
- Forgiving people so that your holding of a grudge becomes more serious to you than whatever the grudge is about.

- Caring for "the least of these" by seeing and serving
  needy or vulnerable people (the sick, children, the elderly,
  the disabled, those racially or otherwise different from
  you, or any type of person you normally struggle to love)
  as if they were Christ himself.

You wouldn't be trying to follow Jesus' teachings to earn anything (as if you were God's employee rather than God's accepted
and loved child), or to avoid anything (as if they were laws and
you were trying to avoid a fine or jail time), or to win anything
(as if you were playing a game). Instead, you would simply be
experimenting to see if the way of life taught by Jesus really
proves, in your experience, to be good and worthwhile—and
whether it increases your confidence in Jesus as a teacher or not.
As you experiment, you might want to keep Jesus' words in
mind: "Anyone who chooses to do the will of God will find out
whether my teaching comes from God or whether I speak on my
own" (John 7:17 TNIV).

Your group may want to explore spiritual formation in the
way of Jesus by experimenting with various spiritual practices
like these:

- *Silence and solitude.* Taking a period of time each day or
  week to be alone and silent, mindful of God's presence, as
  you sit, walk, drive, or kneel.
- *Giving to the poor.* Perhaps keeping a certain sum of money
  in your pocket ready to give it to the first person you
  meet who needs it or raising money for some good cause
  that will help people in need.
- *Fasting.* Going without food for a mealtime or a day or
  even longer.
- *Prayer.* Using the Lord's Prayer—slowly and thought-

fully—once or twice or three times a day or following another plan for regular prayer.[3]

- *Mindfulness.* Learning to be mindful of God (or "practicing God's presence") at least once each day, then once each hour, then more and more frequently, until you are mindful of God's presence for extended uninterrupted periods of time.
- *Gratitude.* Noticing each pleasure and blessing that comes your way, and thanking God for it as a gracious gift.
- *Hospitality.* Sharing meals together in one another's homes as part of your gatherings—or, recalling Jesus "scandalous inclusion" in table fellowship, inviting unexpected people (a stranger, a homeless person, a neighbor, a person of another background, race, or religion) to join you.

You could all agree on a spiritual practice for a week or a month and each week share some of your experiences with it. In all of these ways you would be practicing the way of life of the kingdom of God.

3. *Plot goodness.*[4] At some point, your group should decide to do something to benefit others not included in your group—to somehow express the kingdom of God. Years ago, a group of our friends began collecting used clothing. When we had a couple of car trunks full of clothes, we would drive to a poor neighborhood on a Saturday. Then we'd string clotheslines between some trees in a parking lot and hang or drape all the clothes on the clotheslines. Then we'd run into the apartment buildings and start knocking on doors, telling people there was a surprise outside if they were interested. I'll never forget the thrill of watching scores of people rush out and go shopping for free in their parking lot. If they asked us why we were doing this, we'd simply say, "We want you to know God loves you."

Or maybe you can prepare a picnic and show up in a park in your city where homeless people stay, as my friend Spencer Burke has done in his town. Don't just give them food and leave; stay and let them share in a picnic with your group.

We all know what terrorist cells do. Maybe your group could become the opposite of a terrorist cell, secretly plotting goodness to surprise people with glimpses of God's kingdom: throwing parties, visiting hospitals, giving out flowers, planting gardens, fixing houses for elderly or disabled people, cleaning homes, fixing cars, babysitting for single parents, building playgrounds, cleaning up trashy neighborhoods or streams or roadsides. Whatever you do, you can make it creative and fun—giving people a taste of the kingdom of God through your kindness.

Or maybe you should take on an issue of injustice, as a group of my friends did recently. We are concerned about the genocide occurring in Darfur, so we organized five outdoor worship services in five key locations in Washington, D.C. We called our project "Worship in the Spirit of Justice," and each week, through word and song we praised God as the God of justice who cares for the oppressed, and we called on our nation and its government not to stand idly by while our neighbors' blood was being shed.[5] You could spend a half year learning about a country in need and then do whatever you can to help. (Believe me, as you study the issues, ideas will come to you.) Who knows what a difference you could make?

You might wonder what a group like this should be called. Some might want to call it a study group, a fellowship group, a faith community, a missional community, a lay monastery (a group of laypeople gathering around spiritual practice and mission), a spiritual formation group, or a spiritual conversation group. Some people might eventually want to call a group like this a church— perhaps a microchurch, a minichurch, a house church, or maybe a liquid or organic church. After all, it is a group gathered around Jesus and his message.[6] (Of course, some wouldn't see that as proper.) Some groups might form as Christian education classes within churches—and they could choose to invite some nonchurch friends to join them; the diversity of perspective would benefit everyone. If you want to create some intrigue around your group, call it a "secret group," since you're exploring Jesus' secret message.

If you'd like to share your experiences in such a group or if you'd like to get additional ideas and resources, check out these Web sites: www.emergentvillage.com and www.anewkindofchristian.com.

I would suggest that you conclude your gatherings by joining hands and saying together the prayer Jesus taught his disciples— the prayer we could appropriately call the "prayer of the kingdom." It seems to provide the best words with which to conclude this book:

> "Our Father in heaven,
> hallowed by your name,
> your kindgom come,
> your will be done,
>   on earth as it is in heaven.
> Give us this day our daily bread.
> Forgive us our debts,
>   as we also have forgiven our debtors.
> And lead us not into temptaion,
> but deliver us from the evil one."

For if you forgive men when they sin against you, your heavenly Father will also forgive you, but if you do not forgive men their sins, your Father will not forgive your sins. (Matthew 6:9–15)[7]

NOTES

INTRODUCTION

1. For example, the theological meaning of Jesus' death is central to all streams of Christian thought and life, but since this is a book on Jesus' message, I limit my reflections on his death here to how it relates to his primary teaching theme. Emphasizing one theme is not meant to minimize the other.

2. My friends Steve Chalke and Alan Mann have written a provocative and helpful book with a theme and title similar to this one: *The Lost Message of Jesus* (Grand Rapids: Zondervan, 2003). Along with sharing many of the same critics, we share a common aim: "that this book might provoke thoughtful debate, pose fresh questions and shed a little new light, but more than that, stir our hearts, fire our emotions, and fuel our imaginations" (p. 16).

CHAPTER 1: TROUBLING QUESTIONS ABOUT JESUS

1. If I could have found a graceful and more concise way of putting it, this sentence would have generated the subtitle for this book, which would have been something like this: *The Secret Message of Jesus: His Surprising and Largely Untried Plan for a Political, Social, Religious, Artistic, Economic, Intellectual, and Spiritual Revolution.* Because I already have a reputation for ungainly subtitles, though, we rejected this one in favor of a simpler one.

2. Sharon D. Welch's *After Empire: The Art and Ethos of Enduring Peace* (Minneapolis: Augsburg Fortress, 2004) exemplifies for me one kind of productive and needed interreligious reflection. In terms of Buddhist-Christian dialogue, I think of the Dalai Lama's *The Good Heart: A Buddhist Perspective on the Teachings of Jesus* (Somerville, Mass.: Wisdom, 1998) or Thich Nhat Hanh's *Living Buddha, Living Christ* (New York: Riverhead, 1997). And in terms of Muslim-Christian dialogue, I can't help but think of *Islam, Postmodernism and Other Futures: A Ziauddin Sardar Reader,* edited by Sohail Inayatullah and Gail Boxwell (London: Pluto, 2003), or Irshad Manji's *The Trouble with Islam* (New York: St. Martin's, 2004). What Sardar identifies as the trouble with Western Christianity and Manji identifies as the trouble with Islam could both be radically addressed by a rediscovery and reappraisal of the secret message of Jesus.

Chapter 2: The Political Message of Jesus

1. My friend Jim Wallis explains this distinction in his important book *God's Politics: Why the Right Gets It Wrong and the Left Doesn't Get It* (San Francisco: HarperSanFrancisco, 2005).

2. Much of the historical material here comes from N. T. Wright's writings, including *The Challenge of Jesus* (London: SPCK, 2000). Many of his lectures are available online at www.ntwrightpage.com.

3. Among these theologians and writers who explore the political dimension of Jesus' message are John Howard Yoder, Stanley Hauerwas, N. T. Wright, Jim Wallis, Walter Brueggemann, Walter Wink, Ron Sider, Rene Padilla, Chuck Gutenson, and Tony Campolo.

4. As we will see in chapter 16, the terms *kingdom* and *empire* are problematic today because they carry different connotations than they did in Jesus' day. For our purposes here, I am using the word *empire* to mean "kingdom of kingdoms," not to imply a kind of colonial imperialism.

5. Lee Camp helpfully summarizes the political dimension of Jesus' message: "[The disciples] were not wrong in expecting a real kingdom that would make a difference in human history, politics, and culture. Jesus corrected them not for expecting a kingdom; he corrected them for their false construal of the *kind* of king who would rule the kingdom. . . . That is, they were not wrong for expecting a 'political' kingdom as opposed to a 'spiritual' one. . . . Instead, Jesus announced a kingdom that was *political*—in that 'politics,' in the classic sense, is concerned with the manner in which real communities arrange their affairs. . . . The rule of God was not far off in the heavens, but even then, [it was] invading human history. The kingdom of heaven is at hand'" (*Mere Discipleship* [Grand Rapids: Brazos, 2003], 92).

Chapter 3: The Jewish Message of Jesus

1. Interestingly, early Christian writers did link Jesus with the priesthood of a non-Jew known as Melchizedek, who seemed to represent a kind of organic, pre-Jewish, primal priesthood (see Hebrews 5:5–10). For a fascinating exploration of this subject, see Don Richardson, *Eternity in Their Hearts* (Ventura, Calif.: Regal, 1981).

2. My book *The Last Word and the Word After That* (New York: Jossey-Bass, 2005) explores in an introductory way the history and meaning of the language of hell.

3. Walter Brueggemann calls this prophetic function "prophectic imagination." See *The Prophetic Imagination* (Minneapolis: Augsburg Fortress, 2001).

CHAPTER 4: THE REVOLUTIONARY MESSAGE OF JESUS

1. My book *The Story We Find Ourselves In* (New York: Jossey-Bass, 2003) is devoted to exploring this biblical narrative in more detail.
2. We could also speak of Jesus as a new Joshua—the two names being synonymous in Hebrew—with an expansive mission of reconciliation and healing instead of conquest and destruction.
3. Thanks to Wes White for his insights, which have influenced this chapter.

CHAPTER 5: THE HIDDEN MESSAGE OF JESUS

1. Thanks to Dallas Willard for this language of *interactive relationship*.
2. For more on Jesus' intriguing use of questions see Conrad Gempf, *Jesus Asked* (Grand Rapids: Zondervan, 2003).

CHAPTER 6: THE MEDIUM OF THE MESSAGE

1. For more information on the challenges of speaking (or writing and reading) about God, see Peter Rollins, *How (Not) to Speak of God* (London: SPCK, 2006).

CHAPTER 7: THE DEMONSTRATION OF THE MESSAGE

1. Although I believe that miracles can occur, I don't believe every report of a miracle that I hear, because many reports stem from wishful thinking, self-delusion, exaggeration, and downright fraud. Nor do I believe in miracles on demand, the idea that miracles are guaranteed for anyone who gets the right formula. That would reduce God's power to a mechanism, which means we're again packing God into the predictable boxes of our modern, Western, mechanistic, reductionistic worldview. It would reduce the supernatural to a kind of natural mechanism.
2. For more on my personal spiritual journey, you might want to check out my more personal or confessional books *Finding Faith* (Grand Rapids: Zondervan, 1999) and *A Generous Orthodoxy* (Grand Rapids: Zondervan, 2004).
3. Covert racism may turn out to be harder to eradicate than overt racism.
4. Fyodor Dostoevsky (1821–1881) spoke of the person trapped in a mechanistic worldview who "will always find strength and ability to disbelieve in the miraculous, and if he is confronted with a miracle as an irrefutable fact he would rather disbelieve his own senses than admit the fact. Faith does not . . . spring from the miracle, but the miracle from faith" (*The Brothers Karamazov*, chapter 5).

5. It is interesting to contrast this approach to signs and wonders with the approach of many—not all—so-called healers and miracle workers today.

CHAPTER 8: THE SCANDAL OF THE MESSAGE

1. His response is the polar opposite of the institutional cover-ups of wrong-doing that have been so common in our day.

2. This tension between the kingdom of God as a powerful force—but not a *forceful* or *irresistible* force—comes through in John 3:16–21: "For God so loved the world. . . . Light has come into the world, but people loved darkness instead of light because their deeds were evil" (TNIV). God's love and light—arguably the most powerful forces in the world—can be rejected.

3. Acts 16:16–18 provides a counterexample, where Paul directly confronts a "personal demon." In 1 Corinthians, Paul seems to have a kind of ambiva-lence regarding personal demons. In 8:4–7, he says, "An idol is nothing at all in the world. . . . But not everyone knows this." Then, in 10:19–20, he says, "Do I mean . . . that an idol is anything? No, but the sacrifices of pagans are offered to demons, not to God." Is Paul affirming the reality of demons, or is he merely asserting the misguided intentions of the idol worshiper?

4. I can think of no more chilling a dramatization of this process than the HBO movie *The Conspiracy*, which depicts a group of German officials being "pos-sessed" by the spirit of Nazism.

5. Mohandas Gandhi (1869–1948), having seen the ugly underbelly of Western Christianity in colonialism, once said, "I consider Western Christianity in its practical working a negation of Christ's Christianity."

6. It should be noted that one of the satanic temptations of Jesus was to cut a deal and abandon his work for the kingdom of God in exchange for "all the kingdoms of the world" (Matthew 4:8). This may represent the primal temp-tation of all power.

7. See Bruce Ellis Benson, *Graven Ideologies: Nietzsche, Derrida and Marion on Modern Idolatry* (Downers Grove, Ill.: InterVarsity, 2002).

CHAPTER 9: YOU CAN'T KEEP A SECRET

1. See, for example, Isaiah 60:1–3 or Psalm 117 or the amazingly subversive book of Jonah.

CHAPTER 11: THE OPEN SECRET

1. For an alternative reading, refer to chapter 19.

2. Bishop N.T. Wright explores the relation of Jesus and Paul in *What St. Paul Really Said: Was Paul of Tarsus the Real Founder of Christianity?* (Grand Rapids: Eerdmans, 1997).

3. This radical social outworking of the message of the kingdom is, I think, too seldom appreciated today. See Acts 10:1–11:18; 2 Corinthians 5:16; Colossians 3:11; Galatians 3:28; and Ephesians 2:13–18.

CHAPTER 12: HIDING THE MESSAGE IN NEW PLACES

1. It was a form of Aramaic. See Lamin Sanneh, *Translating the Message: The Missionary Impact on Culture* (Maryknoll, N.Y.: Orbis, 1989).

2. See Sylvia Keesmaat and Brian Walsh, *Colossians Remixed: Subverting the Empire* (Downers Grove, Ill.: InterVarsity, 2004) for a brilliant exploration of this theme in Colossians.

3. Actually, Paul is closer to Jesus in this regard than many realize. Take the book of Romans, where Paul structures his story less as a linear argument and more as a rapid-fire succession of parable-like analogies, images, narratives, and imaginary conversations. He evokes marriages and divorces, slaves and masters, bodies and body parts, pots and potters, along with a number of biblical stories involving characters from Adam to Abraham. Paul proves himself less the lawyer making arguments and more the poet making parables than many people have realized.

CHAPTER 13: GETTING IT, GETTING IN

1. This idea is wonderfully captured in Jill Phillips's song "God Believes in You," on her CD *Writing on the Wall* (Fervent, 2003).

CHAPTER 14: KINGDOM MANIFESTO

1. For two classics on spiritual practice, see Richard Foster, *Celebration of Discipline* (Harper San Francisco, 1998) and Dallas Willard, *Spirit of the Disciplines* (Harper San Francisco, 1991).

2. Dallas Willard, "Jesus the Logician," *Christian Scholars Review* 28, no. 4 (1999): 605–14, available at www.dwillard.org.

3. A Christian apologist of the late second century, Athenagoras, defined the Christian ethos in these terms: "But among us you will find uneducated persons, and artisans, and old women, who, if they are unable in words to prove the benefit of our doctrine, yet by their deeds exhibit the benefit arising from their persuasion of the truth: they do not rehearse speeches but exhibit

good works; when struck, they do not strike again; when robbed, they do not go to law; they give to those who ask of them, and love their neighbors as themselves" (A. Roberts, ed., *The Ante-Nicene Fathers* [New York: Christian Literature Press, 1885], 134).

CHAPTER 15: KINGDOM ETHICS

1. Conventional readings of the kingdom manifesto often make much of how impossibly demanding it is, driving us to despair about ever actually living this way, so that we will faithfully turn to God for mercy. I wholeheartedly affirm the need to turn to God for mercy, but I don't see the manifesto as a call to achieve a kind of pharisaical technical perfection. Instead, this way of life impresses me less as impossibly or oppressively demanding than as healthy, attractive, and liberating. It recalls for me Jesus own words about his ethical teaching (called a "yoke" in his day): "Come to me, all who labor and are heavily burdened, and I will give you rest. Take my yoke upon you, and learn of me, for I am meek and humble in heart, and you will find rest for your souls. For my yoke is easy and my burden is light" (Matthew 11:28–30). For more on "yoke," see *Velvet Elvis* (Grand Rapids: Zonderan, 2005), 40ff. As Dallas Willard says, the cost of discipleship must be compared to the terrible toll of nondiscipleship.

2. For more on this reading of Jesus' manifesto, see Walter Wink, *The Powers That Be: Theology for a New Millennium* (New York: Galilee Doubleday, 1998).

CHAPTER 16: THE LANGUAGE OF THE KINGDOM

1. The quoted words come from Dallas Willard. For more on the translatability of the gospel, see Lamin Sanneh, *Translating the Message: The Missionary Impact on Culture* (Maryknoll, N.Y.: Orbis, 1989).

2. Dr. Grenz, who in recent years became a friend and mentor to me, passed away during the writing of his book. *Theology for the Community of God* (Grand Rapids: Eerdmans, 2000) is a good introduction to his work.

3. The beautiful Shaker hymn "Lord of the Dance" deserves a fresh look and listen in light of the power and beauty of this metaphor.

CHAPTER 17: THE PEACEABLE KINGDOM

1. I would recommend Walter Wink's *The Powers That Be: Theology for a New Millennium* (New York: Galilee Doubleday, 1998) for further study on this vitally important subject. Also, reflection on two films, *The Mission* (1986)

and *To End All Wars* (2001), will stimulate important dialogue on Jesus and violence.

2. Lee Camp, *Mere Discipleship: Radical Christianity in a Rebellious World* (Grand Rapids: Brazos, 2003), 125.

3. Martin Luther King Jr., "Where Do We Go from Here?" annual report delivered at the 11th Convention of the Southern Christian Leadership Conference, 16 August 1967, Atlanta, Ga.

4. Martin Luther King Jr., "The Casualties of the War in Vietnam," speech delivered 25 February 1967, Los Angeles, Calif.

5. Martin Luther King Jr., address delivered in acceptance of Nobel Peace Prize, 10 December 1964, Oslo, Norway.

6. The classic movie *A Few Good Men* serves as a commentary on these situations, as does the more recent real-life torture at the Abu Ghraib prison in Iraq.

7. Sharon D. Welch writes, "We need the courage of those who refuse to serve in unjust situations. We need the presence of the Israelis and Palestinians who demonstrate for peace, declaring, 'We are not each other's enemy.' We need the people in the United States who stand . . . in solidarity with those who suffer and in silent witness to the horror of war. Without such principled objections to war, without such resolute commitment to peace, I would question our humanity. Without other actions, however—without sustained, concerted attempts to institutionalize means of preventing war—I question our creativity and wisdom." She then reminds us of the old dictum: *"Dulce bellum inexpertis*—war is sweet to those who have not experienced it." (*After Empire: The Art and Ethos of Enduring Peace* [Minneapolis: Augsburg Fortress, 2004], 161–62).

8. I am aware that as I write these words, many in the world fear that my country is seeking to revive a new era of colonialism. I share their fear, and I hope that this book may in some small way keep the wind blowing strong against that kind of revival.

CHAPTER 18: THE BORDERS OF THE KINGDOM

1. For more information on Jesus' "table fellowship," see Conrad Gempf, *Mealtime Habits of the Messiah* (Grand Rapids: Zondervan, 2005).

2. Thanks to Wes White of Glasgow, Scotland, for this phrase.

CHAPTER 19: THE FUTURE OF THE KINGDOM

1. I'm not saying here that there are no predictions in the Bible, but rather that

many of the passages that we commonly interpret as such would be better interpreted as warnings and promises.

2. For more on this approach to biblical prophecy, see Craig Hill, *In God's Time: The Bible and the Future* (Grand Rapids: Eerdmans, 2002), and Walter Brueggemann, *The Prophetic Imagination* (Minneapolis: Augsburg Fortress, 2001).

3. For a provacative reading of the Book of Revelation and related topics from a perspective similar in several respects to the one presented in this chapter, see the work of Timothy and Max King (presence.tv).

4. Available at www.christianfutures.com and www.presence.tv. Also, see the seminal work of Andrew Perriman on the kingdom of God and eschatology, available at www.opensourcetheology.net, and in his forthcoming book *The Coming of the Son of Man*. Also see Scot McKnight's important book *A New Vision for Israel: The Teachings of Jesus in National Context* (Grand Rapids: Eerdmans, 1999).

5. Andrew Perriman (www.opensourcetheology.net) provocatively calls our context, after AD 67–70, *post-eschatological.*

CHAPTER 20: THE HARVEST OF THE KINGDOM

1. C. S. Lewis offers four definitions of heaven in *Miracles* (San Francisco: HarperSanFrancisco, 2001), 256–57. For Lewis, the word *heaven* generally includes what we will call resurrection and the intermediate state between death and resurrection. He defines heaven as "the whole Nature or system of conditions in which redeemed human spirits, still remaining human, can enjoy such participation [in the divine life of God] fully and for ever." This unusually broad definition of heaven may in fact be identical or nearly identical to our idea of the kingdom of God in this book, since for Lewis this participation in the divine life of God begins here and now, before death. His emphasis is on a glorious future reality that in a sense invades the present, where ours is more on a glorious present reality that expands into an even more glorious future, but the common ground is significant.

2. *Heaven* sometimes simply means the sky—as in a phrase like "birds of the heavens." But for ancient people, we must remember that the sky (the mysterious source of sunlight and rain) was also seen as the home of God. So it wasn't "simply" the sky. *Heaven* in this sense would bear the same relationship to the "merely physical" atmosphere, sky, or space as *heart* would have to the merely physical biological pump in the chest in a sentence like, "I love you with all my heart." *Heaven* also can be used as a kind of placeholder for God,

as when we say, "Heaven help us," meaning, "God help us." (*Kingdom of heaven* probably works with this meaning.)

3. For more on heaven and its relation to resurrection, see N. T. Wright, *The Resurrection of the Son of God* (Minneapolis: Augsburg Fortress, 2003), especially pp. 417ff.

4. The conventional idea of disembodied souls or spirits is being reappraised these days in theological circles. For a good introduction to this discussion, see Joel Green, ed., *What About the Soul?* (Nashville: Abingdon, 1999).

5. I grapple with this subject in more detail in *The Last Word and the Word After That* (New York: Jossey-Bass, 2005). See especially pp. 115–20.

6. The notion of "white privilege" provides a rare example of modern people acknowledging group responsibility.

7. We mentioned another religious group, the Essenes, in a previous chapter. Their complex views of the afterlife are less relevant here, since they isolated themselves from the rest of Jewish society.

8. For those familiar with postwar, post-Holocaust, post-colonial philosophy and its sensitivity to power, oppression, domination, and injustice, the phrase suggests that Jesus' kingdom aims to deconstruct all other approaches to authority. This could be seen as the most dominating project of all—the ultimate imperialism—if it weren't for the fact that Christ, in the end, will not hold power but will hand it over, let it go, and "subject himself" to God. One thinks of J. R. R. Tolkien's The Lord of the Rings trilogy, which involves this very theme: the cautious holding of power by the meek so it can finally be released and destroyed. This paradoxical approach to power is, as we have seen, at the center of Jesus' life, ministry, and secret message. He is a king who acts like a servant by washing his disciples' feet, who rides a humble donkey rather than a warrior's stallion, who rules not from a throne but from a cross, who brings peace not by shedding the blood of others but by bleeding and suffering himself, who says "the greatest among you is the servant of all," and thus starkly contrasts his understanding of greatness with those who rule by "lording over" others.

9. Walter Wink, *The Powers That Be: Theology for a New Millennium* (New York: Galilee Doubleday, 1998), 64.

10. C. S. Lewis, *Miracles* (San Francisco: HarperSanFrancisco, 2001), 243–44.

11. C. S. Lewis, *The Problem of Pain* (San Francisco: HarperSanFrancisco, 2001), 148–49.

12. C. S. Lewis, *The Weight of Glory* (San Francisco: HarperSanFrancisco, 2001), 25.

13. Interestingly, one of Paul's translations of "in the kingdom" seems to be "in the risen Christ." Clearly, our resurrection has not yet happened; yet for Paul in some way, through the resurrection of Christ it already has: we were in some way raised *with* him. So Paul says, for example, "We were therefore buried with him through baptism into death in order that, just as Christ was raised from the dead through the glory of the Father, we too may live a new life. . . . The death he died, he died to sin once for all; but the life he lives, he lives to God. In the same way, count yourselves dead to sin but alive to God in Christ Jesus" (Romans 6:4–11). "God raised us up with Christ and seated us with him in the heavenly realms in Christ Jesus" (Ephesians 2:6). "Since, then, you have been raised with Christ, set your hearts on things above" (Colossians 3:1). Put differently, we are invited to begin living now the way everyone will someday live in the resurrection, in the world made new. We let our lives be formed not by the past, and not by the present, but by this future that has in some way, through Christ's resurrection, been made present and available now.

14. "A glorious story that never, ever ends" is not the same as a story that ends in timeless stasis, a platonic state where nothing ever happens again. What God hopes to harvest from creation is exactly what most harvests involve: *seeds and fruit.* Whether it's apples or wheat or corn or soybeans, what is harvested is generally the reproductive germ necessary for a future growing season. So the harvest of this world and its history will gather in the good fruit of all times and places—purged of chaff, winnowed of evil—leaving only pure seeds full of new possibilities for a bright future. "The end," then, is not the end of the future but rather its new beginning, having been liberated from the vicious cycles and domination structures of this "present evil age" (Galatians 1:4). Both Jesus and Paul employ another image to convey this ending-as-new-beginning: childbirth (John 16:20–22; Romans 8:22–23). In that metaphor, this universe is in a kind of cosmic labor that will in some way give birth to a new creation. Paul describes the pains and struggles we experience as a sharing in Christ's sufferings—labor pains necessary for giving birth to the kingdom of God in its fullness. These pains, he says, are "light and momentary"—not worth comparing to the "eternal weight of glory" that will be revealed (2 Corinthians 4:17 NIV, KJV, also Romans 8:18).

15. C. S. Lewis, *Mere Christianity* (San Francisco: HarperSanFrancisco, 2001), 137. One might add that the image of everyone wearing crowns resonates with the destruction of the "domination system," evoking a kind of egalitarianism

where all people are equally empowered and free. Similarly, when Peter uses the language "a kingdom of priests," he is suggesting a society in which there is no religious dominance system, since everyone is a priest. Of those who take this imagery of harps, crowns, gold, and pearly gates too literally, Lewis says, "If they cannot understand books written for grown-ups, they should not talk about them." Lewis offers his own fertile imagery of the afterlife in *The Great Divorce* (San Francisco: HarperSanFrancisco, 2001).

16. Lewis, *Weight of Glory*, 38–39.

CHAPTER 21: SEEING THE KINGDOM

1. Huston Smith, *The Soul of Christianity: Restoring the Great Tradition* (San Francisco: HarperSanFrancisco, 2005).

2. C. S. Lewis, *The Weight of Glory* (San Francisco: HarperSanFrancisco, 2001), 397.

3. Frederick Buechner, *Secrets in the Dark* (New York: HarperCollins, 2005), 118.

4. Ibid., 214.

5. Ibid., 214–15.

6. Ibid., 121.

7. Ibid., 122.

8. It is interesting, in this light, that the book of Revelation ends not with people going up to heaven but with the heavenly Jerusalem (the "City of Peace") coming down to earth.

APPENDIX 1: WHY DIDN'T WE GET IT SOONER?

1. Michael Cassidy

2. Thanks to Jo-Ann Badley for this insight into what makes a good interpretation good.

3. By the way, those who believe the so-called Gnostic Gospels offer a more radical way of reading the text should note that those documents are far more "Greek" than the documents we have in the Bible. They generally contain unsituated sayings of Jesus—with little or no narrative—and reinforce the timeless-truths approach to Jesus' message rather than this historically rooted, politically engaged approach.

4. Walter Wink, *The Powers That Be: Theology for a New Millennium* (New York: Galilee Doubleday, 1998), 81, 90.

5. See also Mabiala Kenzo's essay on postcolonialism, available on the website www.anewkindofconversation.com, to be included in a forthcoming book edited by Myron Penner.

6. Charles E. Moore, ed., *Provocations: Spiritual Writings of Søren Kierkegaard* (Maryknoll, N.Y.: Orbis, 2003).

7. Wink, *Powers That Be*, 91.

8. See E. Stanley Jones, *Ghandi* (Abingdon, 1993).

APPENDIX 2: PLOTTING GOODNESS

1. For a rendering of the Bible with special sensitivity to its narrative flow, see *The Voice* (to be released by World Publishing).

2. As you consider whom to invite to your group, consider including people from a variety of racial, ethnic, and religious backgrounds. You'll need to establish clear ground rules, of course. For ideas on good ground rules for diverse groups, see the Simple Spirituality materials available at http://www.off-the-map.org/idealab/articles/id10304-1-ss.html. See also resources available at www.anewkindofchristian.com.

3. Some especially helpful plans for regular prayer can be found at these Web sites: www.explorefaith.org and www.sacredspace.ie.

4. Thanks to my friend Bart Campolo for the delightful phrase *plotting goodness*.

5. See www.worship4justice.org and www.crcc.org.

6. If your group explores this path, you may want to incorporate the practices of baptism and communion, as we briefly discussed in chapter 18. For guidance and resources in forming your group into a more intentional missional faith community or church, check out www.emergentvillage.com.

7. For resources on worship in the Spirit of Justice, see www.anewkind-ofchristian.com.

For bonus material, including a discussion guide and an additional chapter, visit www.brianmclaren.net.